Henley Management College

A World Class Pioneer in Management Education

By

Dan Remenyi

Henley Management College
A World Class Pioneer in Management Education

First edition, May 2015

Cover is reproduced from a water colour painting purchased by the author from the artist Ms A Jennings.

Disclaimer: While every effort has been made by the editor, authors and the publishers to ensure that all the material in this book is accurate and correct at the time of going to press, any error made by readers as a result of any of the material, formulae or other information in this book is the sole responsibility of the reader. Readers should be aware that the URLs quoted in the book may change or be damaged by malware between the time of publishing and accessing by readers.

ISBN printed soft cover: 978-1-910309-80-3
ISBN printed hard cover: 978-1-910309-81-0
ISBN printed hard cover with dust jacket: 978-1-910309-84-1
ISBN ePub: 978-1-910309-82-7
ISBN Kindle: 978-1-910309-83-4

Printed by Lightning Source UK Ltd.

Published by: ACPIL, Reading, RG4 9SJ, United Kingdom,
info@academic-publishing.org

Available from www.academic-bookshop.com

Contents

Contents

Contents

Contents

Table of Photographs

12	Susan Foreman - the most senior academic at the College.	Peter Watson	90
13	A degree awarding ceremony presided over by Mr Bones.	Peter Watson	91
14	Souvenir mug handed out at the last night of the College.	Ben Van Den Assem	100
15	About 200 people came to the last night of the College celebration.	Peter Watson	100
16	Three Principals together in formal academic regalia at the college's 60th anniversary celebrations during the Bones term of office. Stephen Watson was noted for his absence.	Peter Watson	101
17	Greenlands changes hands as one flag is lowered and another is raised (two photos).	Peter Watson	103
18	The modern offices of HBS at the Whiteknights campus.	Dan Remenyi	111
19	University of Reading investment has ensured that that Greenlands remains a highly attractive site.	Dan Remenyi	113
20	On a fine day Greenlands look like it will be there forever.	Peter Watson	114

Acknowledgements

Acknowledgements are normally a list of *thank yous* to people who have been kind enough to help in some way in the production of the book. These generally fall into three groups; those who contributed to the thinking which went into the book, those who read an early version of it and commented and those who helped to prepare the final manuscript.

In this case there are a few more groups.

First of all there are my colleagues who have over many years shared their views with me about how the College was managed. It was certainly an unusual organisation with a peculiar structure and culture.

Then there are a number of people who have been very helpful in re-counting their experiences over the last few years of the College. These were challenging times and it has not been easy for some of these people to re-engage with their memories of these events. In fact some people I approached found it too uncomfortable and actually declined to talk about the College.

Nonetheless, I can say that in general I have received a significant amount of encouragement to tell the story in this book.

Help has been received from a number of individuals who have read the book and commented on it for me and I am most grateful for this.

The final manuscript has been scoured by a number of friends before being formally copy-edited and I hope all the imperfections have been removed.

I do need to state that I am particularly indebted to the Dean of Henley Business School, Professor John Board for giving me access to the small informal archive from which I was able to obtain some useful information from original documents pertaining to the College.

In addition Peter Watson offered me an excellent collection of photographs of the College and Faculty and I have indicated in the Table of Photographs which of these have been used in the book.

Foreword

The idea of an "Administrative Staff College" was proposed during the dark days of the Second World War in recognition of the need to improve British industrial productivity and to manage the turbulence that would follow the end of the War. This College was instituted at Henley within three months of VE day, and the Henley Course was rapidly recognised as a key piece in the new field of management development. As business and organisational education changed over the next decades, Henley also evolved and reconfigured itself. Thus, Henley is both an important part of the UK's educational system and is also an admirable study in innovation and entrepreneurship.

This unique story is told in an engaging way by Dan Remenyi, who has a 25 year association with Henley, and I welcome and indeed recommend the book as a study of our remarkable history, which has led to the creation of the internationally acclaimed Henley Business School.

John Board

Professor and Dean
Henley Business School
University of Reading
August 2015

Sources for this book

This book is based on many different sources of data including but not limited to:-

A number of different College Administrative Staff documents such as course handbooks, brochures, press releases, and memos to mention only a few;

The minutes of meetings of the Court of Governors of the Administrative Staff College and their annual accounts;

Numerous press cuttings from the national and local press;

The Journal of the Greenlands Association;

A number of books written by former College staff members and others (see bibliography);

The book *Henley – The unfinished management revolution*;

Interviews and discussions with staff and former staff from Henley Management College;

Telephone conversations with numerous people including an official of the Privy Council;

The Henley Management College Report of the Governors and the Financial Statements.

The photographs have been sourced as per the Table of Photographs.

About the Author

 Dan Remenyi completed a doctor of philosophy degree at Henley Management College in 1990 and since then has been involved with the College in a number of different ways. For nearly 20 years he has been concerned with teaching some aspects of research methodology as well as supervising a number of research degree candidates.

During his period of association with the College the institution has had four different Principals.

Beyond the College he has held visiting professorships in more than six universities in four countries and has authored or co-authored some 30 books and more than 50 peer-reviewed academic papers. He is currently developing a series of monographs on his educational and working experiences.

Dedication

Dedicated to the hundreds of men and women who worked at Henley Management College over the years and contributed to making it a world class business school and to the tens of thousands of people who attended conferences or seminars or who took a certificate or diploma or a degree at the College.

Preface

On August 1, 2008 Henley Management College based at Greenlands became part of the Henley Business School which was created by combining the business studies faculty of the University of Reading with Henley Management College. In the lead up to this reorganisation the staff at Greenlands had been told that the then current institution which was Henley Management College was no longer viable. This was because it was now necessary for the College to play in a global market and it was therefore essential to merge with a large university in order to be able to compete with giants such as Harvard Business School and other similar institutions.

Henley Management College evolved from the original Administrative Staff College which was incorporated in 1945. From the very beginning it was a world class pioneer in management education in two respects. Firstly it developed syndicate based problem solving orientated mid-career management education and secondly, through distance learning it brought MBA type education to the whole world.

Initially it was a company limited by guarantee and registered as an independent charity, which in the 1970s developed a loose but highly functional association with Brunel University and through this offered a range of degrees. The College was proud of its independence. In its 60 years of operation it delivered a wide range of educational events in the form of degrees, diplomas and certificates to tens of thousands of graduates. Initially it pioneered the syndicate method of executive development with strong emphasis on the development of management competencies. It attracted senior managers to its programmes from all over the world. It was in some important ways responsible for stimulating the establishment of management development institutions and programmes in India, Australia, Philippines, Ghana and other parts of the world. Henley Management College played an important role in understanding how to facilitate competencies in organisations at board of directors level as well as addressing detailed topics such as their highly successful programmes in project management.

The College had obtained a Royal Charter which changed its corporate status and then a few years later it acquired its own degree-awarding powers and was noted for its high degree of innovation in both the educational and research aspects of academe. At its height Henley Management College, which had pioneered the distance learning MBA, was arguably the largest business school in the world. Its programmes were well re-garded in the business world with a number of large organisations adopting a Henley in-house or corporate degree as a standard for their executives. When it moved into the doctoral education business it quickly developed a highly respected DBA programme which is evidenced by the achievements of its graduates.

For many years the College's activities were exceptionally well received by the business community as well as by the public sector and professional bodies both in the United Kingdom and abroad. Although some good research had been conducted at the College over the years it was not known among the academic community for its excellence in this regard.

This is the story of how Henley Management College developed from 1948 and how it came to pass that it was incorporated into the University of Reading 60 years later. It is not intended that every detail of the events that occurred in this period should be recounted here. This is rather my understanding of the more important aspects of the College's journey to becoming Henley Business School. It will be noticed that I have called upon irony from time to time. Some aspects of this story will puzzle readers and at times I have tried to explain some of the conundrums. However as a former Principal of the College recently said, *"There are some mysteries in this story"*.

Dan Remenyi
dan.remenyi@gmail.com
May 2015

Prologue

There are a number of different ways of telling the story of the College. I have chosen to identify the major events which the College experienced between its inauguration in 1945 and its becoming part of the University of Reading in 2008. I have mostly discussed these events in terms of the approaches taken to the College by the various Principals who were, after all, its Chief Executive Officers. I have made every effort to be objective, but as a social scientist I am aware that objectivity is an aspiration which at best will only be partially achieved. I have made some interpretation of these events, but it will be clear to the reader that I have also left much unsaid as I think that this story provides a significant opportunity for readers' interpretations.

There are other ways of recounting what happened to the College and the role it played in the development of management education thinking over the 60 years of its existence. This involves a discussion of how and why attitudes to management education were formed in the 1940s and how they evolved during the subsequent 60 years.

It has been noted that the genesis of the College can be traced back to the thinking of certain distinguished individuals in the United Kingdom during the mid-years of the Second World War who had come to the conclusion that a new approach to the management of organisations was required. It is possible to see these new ideas as a result of events in the early part of the 20th century such as the great catastrophe which we refer to as the First World War, the economic chaos of the inter-war years and then the commencement of the Second World War. Although it is possible to see the First World War through the lens of heroic endeavour and chauvinistic achievement, it is also clear that it was one of the greatest mistakes of human endeavour. It was misconceived at a number of different levels as well as grossly mismanaged. It was not just Gallipoli or the Somme that were horrendous. Mistakes were made time and time again. This has been well articulated by the author of the expression describing the relationship between the fighting soldiers and their leaders as "Lions being led by donkeys".

The hardships endured by so many people all over the world during the interwar years are legion. On the economic front even Roosevelt's New Deal, which was uniquely progressive for its time, was not enough to take his country out of the economic stagnation. There was something more profoundly wrong with the way in which our societies and economies were managed. Grand strategies by political leaders, as well as the great and the good of the land, were no longer considered enough to ensure peace and prosperity. Too many mistakes were being made between the articulation of the strategies and their realisation in the hands of people in organisations. The influential individuals and the important conceptual thinkers in the early years of the 1940s realised that to succeed, countries were going to have to pay attention to preparing individuals to work together in a much more collaborative and thoughtful way than they had ever done before. There was also at this time the realisation that individuals who were not yet top executives had an important role to play in organisations and that they should be helped to develop themselves for future roles in high office.

It was in this environment that the realisation began that midcareer management education within the context of personal development would facilitate improvements in organisational efficiency and effectiveness.

The ideas for these personal developments and organisational improvements were articulated time and again by a number of different individuals who were involved with the College, but they were most clearly stated in Noel Hall's lectures when he was the Ford Distinguished Visiting Professor at New York University in 1958[1]. The book which was published containing these lectures was in fact the manifesto of Sir Noel Hall as Principal of the Administrative Staff College and showed him to be a thinker of considerable depth.

These ideas and the way they were implemented were so relevant that the College had for quite a few years i.e. until the 1970s, a long waiting list of people who wished to be allowed to attend its course[2]. Although this course was modified over the years it was not until the arrival of Professor Tom Kempner that any real change in the College's direction took place.

The pedagogy developed by Hall and refined by Martin-Bates involved attendance at Greenlands to participate in syndicate groups and to attend some lecture sessions. The Masters degree, which was initiated by Kempner, largely followed the tradition of classroom sessions and this meant that degree candidates had to travel to attend lectures and tutorials.

---

[1] A series of three lectures entitled The Making of Higher Executives: The Modern Challenges, which was subsequently published by the School of Commerce, Accounts and Finance, New York University.
[2] Initially there was only one course offered.

By the 1980s it had become obvious that there was a far greater demand for management education than could ever be accommodated by attendance at the College and this led Kempner to launch the Distance Learning MBA. This approach recognised that the learner is the central character in the personal development event and that, provided adequate materials are supplied and that an appropriate learning schedule is agreed, much of what can be gained by attendance at the University can be achieved by the learner largely on his or her own.

The success achieved by this educational initiative could hardly have been foreseen by the College. It was clearly the right idea at the right time and it catapulted the College from a small scale provider of management courses and a not that well attended MBA, to a global player in this field. The Distance Learning MBA effectively converted the College into a fully fledged Business School.

The College was also a leader in another educational development related to the MBA. Traditionally universities would not admit a student to a Masters Degree programme who had not already completed a bachelors degree. By definition a Masters degree was a postgraduate one and therefore only available to graduates. At various universities this rule was not universally applied and there had always been some discretion afforded to Deans and Heads of Departments. The College was early in offering a route to a non-graduate into a Masters degree. This was through the certificate and diploma approach which is discussed in this book. This was controversial at the time as there were many who believed that without a Bachelors degree, which provided a thorough educational foundation, a Master degree was effectively an intellectual mirage.

Certainly the emphasis on pedagogical innovation at the College was most significant and this alone set it apart from other players in the management education field and made its work notable throughout the world. It is not an exaggeration to say that Henley Management College was truly a world class pioneer in the field of management education.

But there are other lenses through which the story of Henley Management College could be told, not the least of which could be the national economic fortunes of the United Kingdom over those years. There are also the different attitudes of successive governments as well as the developments of education in the Commonwealth and elsewhere abroad. The amount of international attention the College received in the early years and the setting up of separate Administrative Staff Colleges in a number of other countries is testimony to how important the College was. There is also a research perspective. The College undertook or was involved with a number of significant research initiatives, one of the more important being conducted by Meridith Belbin and his team. There is much to be said about this but that aspect of the College is beyond the scope of this book.

This book is but one window through which to reflect on a wide subject. There are many other potential windows which may one day be opened.

Chapter 1

Setting up an Administrative Staff College

1.1.   Henley Management College's success

It is interesting to reflect on how it is possible to be associated with an institution for quite a long time without really understanding what the factors are which drive the success of that body. If I had been asked as recently as a couple of months ago *Why was Henley Management College the great success that it was?* I would have answered with words like those used by many people who frequently spoke about Henley, *"It is highly regarded by business people"*. But this answer is not of much value as it begs another question which is, *"Why is Henley so well regarded by business people?"* Of course this is not a simple question to answer. There was a striking attractiveness of the location and the facilities of the College and these played an important part in its success. There was a long history of the College's hospitality. It welcomed visitors and often treated them to an exceptional lunch. Invariably visitors left the College with a good impression of it. But I now think that more than either of these two issues there was an underlying factor of much greater import which was that Henley Management College had been built and developed over a period of more than 60 years by a solid stream of significant innovations in the realm of management education. It now seems to me that the College's real driver of success was its ability to innovate and the entrepreneurial spirit associated with these innovations. In fact the issue of the College's ability to come up with new ideas and new ways of serving the management education market had been pointed out to me some years before in conversation with Professor Bernard Taylor, who was for many years Henley's leading academic in corporate strategy and business policy. Discussing the College's application for degree-awarding powers Bernard pointed out that the Department of Education would have given the College much credit for the long stream of innovations it had produced over many years.

It is indeed difficult to operate a business school successfully. It was especially difficult in the case of Henley Management College which had continual change firmly ensconced in its collective DNA. To stay a leader in this field it was necessary for the institution to radically reinvent itself a number of times over the years. It is a great credit to all the hundreds of men and women who worked there over the 60 odd years of its existence that they were so successful. A measure of this success may be understood by the claim the College could make on its 50th anniversary:-

> *at any one time there are 10,000 managers working with Henley in or from more than 80 countries and that includes the alumni which is influential and spread over the globe[3].*

There are few, if any, other business schools in the world which could make such a claim.

The path to this success was difficult and as previously stated what made the College such a success was not necessarily clearly understood by all the people involved with the institution. To obtain a full appreciation of Henley Management College it is necessary to tell the story from the beginning and to reflect a little on what is meant by a business school and management education. In general these issues are spoken about rather glibly with many implied assumptions which on investigation are not necessarily correct.

1.2.   In the very beginning

In the book written about the College in 2006 by Rundle it states, "British management education began at Henley[4]". This is at best only partly true as the United Kingdom has a long tradition of successful management both in civil society and in the military. The Empire simply did not run itself. Great business and industrial institutions like Lever Brothers and Imperial Chemical Industries prospered for decades. It may well be the case that in earlier times we relied on natural management or leadership talent, but it is unlikely that this was done without careful consideration, encouragement and instruction from individuals who mentored those young people who were showing promise. Education does not only mani-

---

[3]Internal Henley Management College document
[4]Henley – The unfinished management education revolution, 2006, by David Rundle for Henley Management College.

fest itself in a classroom or a syndicate group but also in personal mentoring and coaching. In fact it is sometimes argued that the best education comes from a combination of experience and careful reflection thereon. Management education was certainly not new to Britain when Henley was established.

The Rundle comment reminds me of the type of misleading information I was given in my first lectures on management which was that management structures were invented in the 19th century in order to cope with the complexity of the organisations which came about due to the building of the railroad from the east coast to the west coast of the United States of America. What a peculiar idea that is! At the same time I was informed that project management had been invented in order to cope with the development of the Polaris missile project. One wonders how the Roman Empire stretching from Scotland to Syria was managed without structure or how the pyramids were built without the notion of project management. Reflection reveals that management has been a part of human existence for millennia, at least since we began to live in towns. On the other hand it is true to say that by the second quarter of the 20th century there was a growing recognition in certain circles in the UK that there was room for improvement as to how organisations were being operated. This was largely driven by growing international competition.

It is correct to say that Henley Management College under the title of the Administrative Staff College was the first to offer formal mid-career management development programmes in the United Kingdom. To use the language of the times this education was delivered in the form of 12 week residential courses and they came about as a result of the realisation by a small group of forward-looking individuals in the early years of the Second World War that the voices of people such as Lyndell Urwick and Mary Parker Follett should be listened to and that there would be considerable value in changing the way organisations functioned. The realisation that this was necessary seems to have come about because of experiences in the two world wars as well as the stunning inability of business and industry to cope during the great depression. It appears that by 1941 it was beginning to be understood that it was necessary for individuals within British industry, commerce, civil service, trade unions as well as men in active military roles, to understand organisational processes and work more closely together if the war was to be won and if prosperity was to be achieved in a post-war Britain.

For the past 12 months a group has been studying a plan to found a National Administrative Staff College. Its conclusions have been fortified by discussions with over 250 leaders representative of almost every side of national life-members of the Government, of both Houses of Parliament, from Commerce and Industry, Trade Associations and Trade Unions, the Fighting and Civil Services, Local Government and the Universities. Tentative proposals have been submitted to the Minister without portfolio who is in charge of reconstruction and have been discussed by his advisory committee.

In a recent Report the Select Committee on National Expenditure has endorsed the value of the group's ideas by recommending Staff College training for the Civil Service.

The members of the group have prepared a short statement of their views on proposals as a contribution to a question which is now of general public interest. Some of them are occupying official positions, they must remain anonymous. But further enquiries may be addressed to:

The Honorary Secretary,
London, WC1
January 1st, 1943.

Exhibit 1: An extract from a pamphlet which was created by the original small group of interested influential individuals who conceived of the idea of an Administrative Staff College. The model they proposed was heavily influenced by the already well established Army Staff College.

A number of influential people began to meet, initially at their clubs in London, to discuss how business and management education in British society might be developed to play really important roles in the country especially when the hostilities had ceased. There were a number of people involved in these discussions which took place during some of the darkest years of the war, but only a few names have been recorded. The best known of these is probably Lyndall Urwick who was already a well-established figure in management and who went on to be a management thinker of global standing. It is interesting to note that Urwick was highly influential in the establishment of the College but that he fell out with the men who actually established the College and therefore did not play a direct part in creating this entity at Greenlands itself[5]. But it was at least in part due to Urwick that the name by which the management college close to Henley-on-Thames, The Administrative Staff College, was known. As well as being an Oxford scholar Urwick had served in the Army during the First World War and had been a Staff Officer. As a Staff Officer he was aware of the ongoing education that army officers received and he believed it was this type of continuous exposure to personal development which was required in other walks of life in British society. He therefore regarded it as appropriate that the new institution which was to be created should be called the Administrative Staff College. It is also worth pointing out that at this time the word administration was used in a similar way to how we use the word management today. This name worked well for the College especially in the immediate postwar period when everyone was aware of how well educated the officer corps in the fighting services were and it was to take Henley quite a few years to move away from its original name, the Administrative Staff College, and to adopt its final title, Henley Management College.

While delving into some old papers at the College I came across an interesting ten page booklet, dated January 1, 1943, describing the idea behind the College and how it should function. This unpretentious little booklet which is smaller than A5 and consists of about 1500 words provides a surprisingly comprehensive description of the aims and the proposed modus operandi of the College. I was struck by how modest the author or authors of this document were in describing what was such a major idea for the improvement of organisational efficiency and effectiveness in the United Kingdom.

This booklet points out that 250 opinion leaders in British society were consulted about the need for a new approach to management education. At any time this is a large number of individuals with whom to hold conversations and it was especially the case in 1942. Clearly there was some urgency associated with the need to create a new institution to deliver a better form of management education. Furthermore there was obviously

---

[5] Urwick insisted that the programme of management education which was under discussion at that time should be at least 12 months in duration. The other members of the discussion group believed that this was too long and that a course of 12 weeks' duration was the maximum length which could be offered. The argument was that there was so little management talent in organisations in the United Kingdom at that time that no one could afford to be absent from their jobs for a whole year. Urwick was non-negotiable on this issue and therefore withdrew from the discussion group.

substantial agreement that a management college should be created and the group, which referred to themselves as the investigating committee, continued to canvass support and finance. By 1945 they were in a position to take the first steps in establishing the management education institution they envisaged and the Administrative Staff College was incorporated in October of that year as a not-for-profit company limited by guarantee. The members of the investigating committee who had been engaged in the discussions during the war years then became members of the Court of Governors, with Geoffrey Heyworth becoming the Chairman, and the College was on its way. The incorporation was followed by an announcement in The Times[6] newspaper which stated:-

The British may reasonably suppose themselves to have some natural talent for administration. They have handled not unsuccessfully a number of considerable enterprises, including an Empire. But their habit has been to do this work without much formal preparation or theorising, making perhaps some acknowledgement to the art but little of the science of administration.

Although this statement recognises "the science of administration" it was not their intention to concentrate too much on this aspect of the subject. The statement in The Times went on to say:-

The curriculum will include some advanced technical instruction. But the greater part of the work will be in small discussion groups and in "syndicates," [sic] designed to train the student in the analysis of his own experience, and in the treatment of practical problems.

Although Henley celebrates 1945 as the year in which it was founded, the first Course only began in 1948. There was much work to be done between the incorporation of a legal entity and being able to open the doors to a cohort of managers wishing to experience midcareer management development.

---

[6] Education in the common tasks of large-scale management, Project for higher training, Hetherington, Sir Hector JW, writing in The Times, November 7 1945.

1.3.   Getting started

The amount of work involved in developing the concept of the Administrative Staff College into a functioning educational entity was truly daunting. There were four main sets of issues to be addressed which were:-

- what type of education and experience would the College provide to those who attended its course;
- where would the College be located;
- how would the operation of the College be funded and;
- how would the College find members to attend its courses.

The first of these was by far the most difficult as it went to the very heart of what this management education initiative was about. It was clear from the outset that the Administrative Staff College would not operate in a similar way to a university. In fact the founding fathers wanted to distance themselves from what they regarded as traditional academic practice. There were a number of good reasons for this including the fact that the activities of the College were being aimed at midcareer individuals and that it was unlikely that such people would be prepared to put themselves through the talk and chalk experience provided by normal university education. What the universities offered was seen as being appropriate to young men and women immediately after school, but not to mature individuals who were in their 30s or early 40s as would be those who attended the College courses.

1.4.   The syndicate method

It was the intention of the College to admit only individuals who were nominated by their employers for this type of special midcareer education. The individuals who would be nominated were people who were regarded as high potential employees who had already achieved some considerable status in their working life and who were likely to become "captains of industry" in due course. There was no former academic requirement for admission to a College course. During the discourse among the initiating committee it was pointed out that some of the people who would attend a College course might have left school at 14 or 15. They would come from all levels of society and therefore might not yet have acquired all the necessary social graces normally found in the higher echelons of organisations and it was thought that the College should address some of these issues during the courses[7].

Philosophy of self development

Part of the philosophical underpinning of the syndicate method was expressed by Sir Hector Hetherington who was Principal and Vice Chancellor of Glasgow University who wrote:-"*The time comes in 8, 10 or 15 years when, having learned and practised his calling, a man does well to take some little time from action and think about what he is doing and why and how he is doing it. This is apt to be the most fruitful educational phase of all.*" Although rather pompously expressed it is hard to deny that there is some validity in this thought.

Self development requires time to reflect on where one has come from and what one is aiming to achieve.

So the College needed to adopt a different route to management education and it was decided to follow what was referred to as the *syndicate method or approach.* The syndicate approach meant that each course of 60 people would be split into six groups of 10. The education experience provided would be based around tasks conducted by individuals working within these groups. Initially there was no detailed syllabus but rather sets of objectives which were given to the groups. There were few lectures offered by the faculty, which in those days were referred to as the Directing Staff (DS), but occasional subject experts were invited.

1. A modern day version of the syndicates group which has remained an important aspect of courses at Henley.

---

[7] This was one of the reasons that formal black tie dinners were held.

However each group had a faculty mentor who was also a DS and who would effectively live with the group for the duration of the course and provide a full range of practical and theoretical advice. These mentors were expected to be generalists who could offer help on any of the topics covered by the course as well as the wellbeing of the course members while they were resident at the College.

Getting above specialisation

The spirit of the Course was to get above specialisation. It was argued that there was adequate training and development opportunities for accountants and other specific corporate functions but nothing for general management. This was largely true and it was this vein of demand which the College was able to serve so successfully.

This meant that the Director of Studies and the other Directing Staff were chosen not for their subject competence but rather for their ability to be able to deliver insights about the challenges facing the highest level of management.

Each member of a syndicate was required to act as its chairperson at some time during the 12 week course and thus group leadership skills would be learnt[8]. Syndicates had to present to the whole course and thus formal presentation skills were also learnt.

The primary learning impetus came from the interaction of individuals in the syndicate groups, who would share experiences with one another and reflect on what they were hearing from each other and the work they were doing together. The richness of the interaction within the groups was ensured by the diversity of the backgrounds of the individuals. The groups were carefully constituted so that there would be a mix of people from industry, commerce and the civil service. Occasionally there was a representative from a trade union and/or the military. This mixing of people was considered of central importance to the syndicate method as it was believed that the cross-fertilisation would result in a rich educational experience for all concerned. Thus a material amount of time was spent ensuring that there was adequate diversity within each syndicate group.

It is important to note that in order to be accepted on a course an individual had to face an acceptance interview during which he or she was tested for suitability. It is worth pointing out that although the courses were

---

[8] Origin, Purpose and the Experience of the Opening Years, An Occasional Paper, The Administrative Staff College, November 1950.

open to both men and women, the number of women attending was very small indeed. In the first 20 years less than one per cent of course members were women. It would take many years before women would have access to or play a significant role in any aspect of management education.

There were also places reserved for individuals from overseas and special arrangements were made for offering them a place on a course.

The syndicate groups would meet continually on their own but they would also come together in plenary sessions where members of a syndicate group would present work produced by their group to the whole course and this would be discussed openly with the Directing Staff which often included the Principal. The work would be intense and the course members were required to be in residence and to apply themselves to their tasks right throughout the day. Course members were only allowed a minimum amount of personal time to be with their families during the 12 week course.

Occasionally specialised lectures would be given and these would be delivered by invited experts, often from important institutions in the City, as it was not the College's intention to develop or employ its own team of international experts. This concept of using outsiders was further developed in later years and eventually constituted a group of many contractors and associate faculty, which became the bedrock of how the College conducted its business into the 21st century.

The syndicate method was in a sense a participative problem-orientated action learning type programme where there was a high degree of direct involvement by the learners rather than sitting and listening to a sage upon a stage, as the traditional academic method is sometimes described. In its time the syndicate method was quite revolutionary.

This type of education, which was intended to stimulate an individual's own interests in his or her personal development, did not lend itself to traditional evaluation and therefore there was no attempt to examine the course members in any way. It was possible for a nominating organisation to make enquiries of the Principal's office as to how a particular individual had got on while at the College[9]. However it was understood that

---

[9] Today there could be ethical issues involved in a practice of secretive evaluation.

personal information would only be released with the permission of the individual concerned.

By the way this approach was to a large extent a copy of how the British Army conducted their executive development programmes in their Staff College for senior officers.

The syndicate method has its supporters but it is not universally recognised as an ideal way of conducting educational events. Members of syndicate groups have complained that some of the time the group spends in discussing a topic amounts to little more than the blind leading the blind and that their learning could have been substantially improved by more expert guidance and input. Over the years the College reduced the amount of time spent employing the syndicate method and introduced more formal lectures and other educational events and exercises.

There was another important pedagogical innovation which was introduced alongside the syndicate groups and that was the practice of having the groups write biographies. These were in-depth group studies of significant individuals who had made a major contribution to their society. The groups could choose almost anyone they wished. The brief given by the College was that the biography should make some assessment of the context, the career and character of the personality studied and draw lessons which might be of use in today's world. These biographies were the College's equivalent of case studies of personalities and what they had to do to achieve that for which they had become famous. This required the members of a syndicate group to work closely together not only in researching the facts for the biography but also in assessing what was significant in the personality and the circumstances of the person being studied.

What is important to note is that in the 1940s the idea of allowing a manager 12 weeks' absence to attend a personal development course was nothing less than revolutionary. Management education was not really on the corporate or organisational radar and it was especially difficult to have organisations agree to release high potential individuals upon whom they were clearly dependent. However the novelty of the proposed course won the day and many organisations subscribed to the College.

1.5. Where might the College be located?

12 weeks in a riverside mansion
There was no doubt a certain degree of attractiveness associated with the idea of spending 12 weeks way at Greenlands, in a Thames-side mansion developing one's management potential. Admittedly the conditions in the house were not great, but then the expectations of the post war workforce were low and the prospect of self improvement meant that sacrifice was not totally unexpected. Everyone loved their time at Greenlands and so was born the idea of the Henley Experience.

There was considerable debate among the initiating committee as to where the College should be located. It was decided at an early stage that the Administrative Staff College should be a national entity and therefore in some sense centrally located. However it was unclear as to whether the institution would be better served by being in the centre of a city or by having a tranquil rural setting. In the event this debate was settled by fortuitous circumstances. It came to the attention of the initiating committee that Viscount Hambleden's riverside residence two miles from Henley-on-Thames would be available. The Hambledens had several homes and the one located on the bank of the Thames, known as Greenlands, was on offer. During the war years Greenlands had been used as a recuperation centre by Great Ormond Street Hospital and the Hambledens had decided that they no longer desired this building as their residence.

At this time Greenlands was not in the best of condition and it was going to be an expensive exercise to restore it to the state it had been in its former days. Viscount Hambleden therefore initially offered Greenlands on a lease to the College's initiating committee free of charge provided the College maintained the property and the grounds. It was however quickly decided that it was more appropriate to ask for a peppercorn rent which was set at £25 per year. This was to be done through a 21 year lease with renewable clauses after each seven year period.

Greenlands was a traditional stately home originally owned by WH Smith, the Victorian newsagent[10]. WH Smith was so successful that he

---

[10] Referring to WH Smith as a Victorian newsagent dates back to a reference in Jerome K. Jerome's humorous novel set on the river Thames called Three Men in a Boat (To Say Nothing of the Dog), published in 1889. Jerome makes reference to Greenlands and its owner who is referred to as a newsagent. By this time the Smith business empire was

was attracted into the Disraeli Government and held a number of important state offices including that of First Lord of the Admiralty[11]. It is said
that when Smith was proposed to Queen Victoria for this maritime post
she responded that she had no objection provided the Navy would accept
a man of the middle classes. Smith became such a successful figure in the
government of his time that on his death his widow was raised to the
peerage as Viscountess[12] Hambleden.

The offer made to the College by Smith's grandson, the 3rd Viscount
Hambleden, was indeed a generous one and the College was fortunate to
have access to Greenlands. But when it came to signing the lease there
were members of the Court of Governors who felt the offer might be too
generous and there could be some difficulties ahead, especially if the
Viscount was to die prematurely. Consequently the College took out a
life insurance on the Viscount and also invited him to join the Court of
Governors. In the event the Viscount died on March 31, 1948, the same
day as the first College course began and the College therefore obtained
the substantial payout which was traditionally said to have made an important contribution to its ability to purchase Greenlands a few years
later.

In the first years of the College preparation of the building for the first
intake of course members was of great importance. As mentioned the
College was not in a great state of repair. In the years that followed the
war there were shortages of all sorts of items and commodities and the
College struggled to find the materials it required to bring the facilities up
to the necessary level. There were issues related to heating, catering and
to the preparation of an adequate number of bedrooms so that the course
could be residential. In general, course members had to share rooms with

---

extensive and included a number of different types of enterprise within the book and
newsprint trade.

[11] This appointment of Smith, a true landlubber, to the post of First Lord of the Admiralty
was sufficiently unusual for Gilbert and Sullivan to include an aria in their operetta HMS
Pinafore, "Stay close to your desk and never go to sea And you may be the ruler of the
Queens Navy". Smith was so successful that he went on to become Lord Warden of the
Cinque Ports which is regarded as a high honour indeed.

[12] A Viscount is a middling rank peerage which comes between an Earl and a Baron. It
can be awarded as either a life peerage or on a hereditary basis. Queen Victoria awarded it
in the hereditary form to Mrs Smith. Writing from Balmoral Castle Queen Victoria expressed her *"deep sense of the service your beloved Husband rendered to me and to his
country"*. Awarding a peerage to the widow of a leading figure was not unique as George
Canning's widow had already been elevated to the peerage in similar circumstances.

some rooms accommodating even three or four course members[13]. Nonetheless all these challenges were faced and overcome at least to some extent by the time the College opened its doors for its first course.

2. The main building at Greenlands as it is today. In 1946 the building was covered in war time camouflage which was only removed in the mid 1960s.

Harry Slater points out in his book, *Henley at Greenlands*[14], that a considerable amount of energy was spent during the early years of the College in raising the funds necessary to improve the buildings. It has been no mean task to take a Victorian stately home and to re-mould it into a modern world class educational facility. Funding the development and the maintenance of the buildings and the beautiful grounds took a considerable amount of energy from the College's Principals.

It is interesting to reflect on the fact that there was little science in the decision as to where to locate the College other than to be close to Lon-

---

[13] The Administrative Staff College, Greenlands, Henley-on-Thames, appeal document, undated, approximately 1962.

[14] Published by Henley in 1988 Harry Salter wrote an interesting account of the House at Greenlands and an account of the first 40 years of the College.

don, but it was rather the generosity of a Viscount who had one house more than he really needed. As a result the College was able to claim in its first prospectus that it was located in "an agreeable Thames-side country house". It is hard to imagine what the College might have been if the founding fathers had located it elsewhere. The image of the solid old mansion house is so integrated into the College's persona that it began to represent what it stood for. In the same way the rich green colour of the College and the oak leaf emblem came to symbolise management growth and development.

1.6. Funding the College

Money and the College

The College seems to have been founded and run for the first 25 years with little reference to any cost accounting. It seems that the fee of £150 which covered the whole 12 weeks may have been established because it was a round number. The fact that the exact costs were not covered was not discovered or highlighted until after the event and a catch up financial strategy was then implemented. This is a remarkable approach for an administration or management college.

During the discussions of the initiating committee[15] it was mentioned a number of times that a budget should be created. It was not possible to commence this exercise until a location for the College had been found as this determined a number of the costs that would be involved in moving forward. However it had been established sometime before then that an appeal would be made for funds from influential individuals and organisations. The appeal was on the basis of asking for covenanted subscriptions i.e. annual sums of money to be paid to the College over a period of time. The initial appeal money was to get the College going and to fund some of the obvious building improvements and additions required. Then it was thought that the College would be self-sustaining through a combination of the fees payable for attendance at the College and the cash flow from the covenanted subscriptions. In retrospect the amount aimed at by the appeal was far too low and the College was to become constrained relatively quickly by the lack of funding.

The appeal did not take long to generate some cash flow and there were adequate funds to be able to appoint a Principal in August 1946, thereby

---

[15] As mentioned previously this was mostly an informal group of business people, but included civil servants and others who met during the war years to discuss how to improve the post-war economy through the delivery of formal management education.

beginning the serious work of turning the idea of an Administrative Staff College into a reality. However the College was never especially well-endowed from a financial point of view and therefore money was continually an issue which required the ongoing attention of the Principal and the Court of Governors.

Useful to attend the College

What was different about 1948 was that the Second World War resulted in an increased awareness of the need to be fair in certain walks of life. This did not mean that the class system had broken down or that it didn't help to be well connected to a member of the establishment. It was clearly a great advantage to have gone to the right school and to have an Oxbridge degree. But it had become easier to advance in organisations through talent, hard work and a desire to climb to the top of the corporate ladder. Being prepared to subject oneself to a 12 week intensive management education course meant that you were serious about preparing to make an important contribution to your organisation.

The appeal attracted one particularly important donor in the form of the Nuffield Foundation which provided the College with the sum of £10,000 over five years for the purposes of offering bursaries to organisations who were not able to afford the fees[16]. The fee was initially set at £150, payable in advance by the nominator, and this sum of money covered tuition, books and papers, as well as all residency costs. Using an Internet inflation calculator it appears that £150 in 1948 was equivalent to £5000 in 2014. It is difficult to assess how expensive this fee appeared to the organisations who wished to avail themselves of the management education provided, but more will be said about this later.

1.7. Members to attend its courses

In the years leading up to the establishment of the College many influential individuals in business, the civil service and other walks of life had been consulted. All of these people had given support to the idea of creating an institution which would deliver mid-career management development. It was therefore a question of how to inform these people of when the College would begin its courses. This was done in a number of ways, one of which was to receive favourable coverage from the establishment press.

---

[16] Fees were not paid by individuals but by the corporate entities which nominated them. In the immediate post-war period there were firms who would struggle to pay the £150 and the College wanted the course to be available to the widest constituents possible.

But as soon as the courses began the feedback from the members was exceptionally good and the demand for the courses grew rapidly. Using modern terminology it would be correct to say that the message concerning the new management education and experience delivered by the Administrative Staff College went viral.

1.8.   Learning-by-doing

In the early years of the College there is a clear sense of adventure on the part of the founding fathers. They had the pioneering vision needed to create the concept; they successfully tested the concept against a substantial number of influential individuals who were able to give them support; they identified an attractive location for the College at a price which they felt that it would be able to bear; with the help of the Principal the underpinning pedagogy was conceived; they found the funds required and they made their vision happen. And all of this was done for the betterment of management education in the United Kingdom.

The founding fathers were learning how to build the College as they went along and this was necessary because no one had ever built a College quite like this before. Many subsequent educational developments are grafted onto already established institutions. This is certainly the case with business schools which are invariably adjuncts to already established universities. But for the Administrative Staff College this was not the case. Everything had to be worked out *ab initio* and the result was without doubt a great achievement.

But getting something going as opposed to creating a sustainable future are two quite different tasks and it may well be that the founding fathers of the College did not pay adequate attention to the long term future. On the other hand business theorists often point out that the average life of business organisations has traditionally been around 40 years. What was created in 1948 by the founding fathers (Hall and Heyworth, to be introduced to readers later) lived on for longer than that.

1.9.   The severity of the challenge

Looking back at the creation of the College in the mid-1940s, it is rather easy to lose sight of how difficult it was to establish such an institution. There is good reason why there had not previously been formal management education in the United Kingdom and one of the reasons was down to the considerable debate as to whether it was possible or not to teach management, especially in a university setting. It was common to hear discussion about the conundrum, "Are managers born or can they be made?" And if managers could be made then it was quite unclear who should be involved in such processes.

This issue was explicitly addressed by Sir Noel Hall when he gave his first lecture as the Ford Distinguished Visiting Professor at New York University in 1958. Hall said and wrote[17]:

> *Perhaps the most remarkable thing is that we are any of us here at all this afternoon in this place to consider this particular topic. Twenty years ago it would have been unthinkable that the process of making higher executives should be discussed at all, and certainly not in an academic setting. They were made in heaven or hell, God's creatures or the Devil's, according to political persuasion. Maybe they just grow'd like Topsy, but the process was not opened to a systematic discussion. It was in 1943 the two initiatives were taken which showed that all this was altering. In that year the War Production Board in Washington asked the Harvard School of Business Administration to develop a special course for those on the way to becoming higher executives for special award assignments, and a distinguished advanced management program at Harvard is today the result. In the same year a group of individuals concerned with deficiencies in British management in the '30s and the stresses and strains which were likely to accompany post-war' redeployment of resources in the United Kingdom were developing their ideas. This led in 1945 to the formation of the Administrative Staff College, which in a rather different way from the Harvard Program plays a modest part in the whole process of making higher executives in the United Kingdom and elsewhere.*

---

[17] Hall N, (1958), The Making of Higher Executives: The Modern Challenge, School of Commerce, New York University,

3. One of the enduring symbols of the College is a Cedar of Lebanon tree which stands between the main building and the river. It is estimated to be over 200 years old.

It was clear from the outset that management could not be taught in the same way as it is possible to teach the Laws of Thermodynamics or the causes of the French Revolution. Although it may not have been expressed in such straightforward terms, what was really being said by those who were developing the College was that management could be learnt by those who were willing to engage in a programme based on discourse, reflection, action to solve problems, and evaluation. As the objective of the College was to develop individuals for future higher executive roles it was necessary to address the issue of self development which was every bit as controversial as the notion of "making" managers. Self development is about moving from a current level of ability to a more comprehensive one and requires the individual concerned to be self-aware in a number of different ways. Although mentors can help with this process it really has to be learnt by the individual for him or herself from experience and thus some sort of action learning is required.

Addressing these particularly difficult issues is what the Administrative Staff College at Henley-on-Thames undertook when it was set up and it made a great success of this highly daunting task.

Setting up an
Administrative Staff College

Chapter 2

The First Principal

2.1. The Principal – N F Hall

Mr Noel Hall was appointed Principal of the Administrative Staff College in August 1946. According to David Rundle he was not the first choice of the Chairman of the Court of Governors who wanted a man with more practical rather than academic experience, and it is suggested that he was appointed to this post as much for his frankness as for anything else. Hall had been a Professor of Political Economy at University College London and therefore had impeccable academic credentials. He had Masters degrees from both Oxford and Princeton. As previously mentioned it was not the College's intention to follow a highly academic approach to its management education. Hall had other important attributes including being well-connected in important circles due to the type of post he held during the war period. He was able to secure a high degree of visibility for the College among people of influence as well as a substantial amount of visibility in the establishment press. Hall arranged a visit by the Prime Minister in 1948 and in 1957 the Queen's Consort, Prince Philip, The Duke of Edinburgh paid the College a visit.

In addition Hall's wartime work had made him pragmatic in his outlook towards management and he took the view that mid-career management education should not have an intense academic orientation but rather it should be as grounded as possible and that it should be focused on the direct personal needs of the individuals attending courses at the College.

Hall was not a man of great physical stature; in fact in most photographs he is one of the shorter individuals in the picture. Nor was Hall a man who generally dressed smartly. However, in all the photographs of him he exudes an air of quiet confidence. He was a man who knew precisely what he was doing.

When one looks at all the challenges the College faced in post-war Britain one wonders why anyone would have taken on such a job. Hall must have been intellectually, emotionally and physically quite a hardy individual. He had all the problems of sorting out the modus operandi of the courses while also having to find what they called the Directing Staff to operate the events. It is not clear from the documents available where the boundaries of the function of the Principal were. Initially it had been suggested that the College should have a President and a Principal. This proposition envisaged a President who would be responsible for all external matters through which the College interfaced with the outside world, and a Principal who would direct all the internal matters for the proper functioning of the institution. However, this route was not followed and these two functions were combined into the one office of Principal. It does appear that there was no explicit statement of how the Principal would work alongside the Chairman of the Court of Governors. The only reference made to this is by Harry Slater in his book, where he mentions in passing that Hall and Heyworth had to work closely together. This of course relates to the College governance although the term was not in common use at that time.

The new Principal had to raise the money to fund the operation and he had all the wonderful challenges related to finding the necessary government licences to acquire the materials needed to make Greenlands into an acceptable venue for management education. In the photographs of the buildings at that time it can be seen that Greenlands had been painted in camouflage colours and the buildings were not fully returned to the pristine white they are today until 1964. Incidentally on the question of this camouflage it has been said that Greenlands was "decorated" in this way for fear of being bombed by the Luftwaffe. Why the German war machine would want to divert a bomber to attack this single stately home on the banks of the Thames 2 miles outside of Henley is not clear. And on top of this, aerial bombing during the Second World War was notoriously inaccurate and therefore it would have been unlikely that Greenlands could have been a target in this way. It has also been said that after the war it was discovered amongst Hitler's personal papers that he had identified Greenlands as a potential residence for himself after his armies had conquered the United Kingdom[18]. The camouflage paint is a rather inter-

---

[18] It has also been said that Senate House in Malet Street in London was not bombed as Hitler believed that it would make a Reich Chancellery.

esting reflection on how resources can be misdirected during a war and the story about Hitler seems like an entertaining proto-myth[19].

It turned out that Hall was a particularly appropriate appointment and under his leadership the College certainly flourished.

2.2. The academic faculty staffing model

Hall introduced an academic faculty staffing model unusual for the time, which was based on a minimum number of full-time permanent employees and the use of external specialists where appropriate. This allowed him to control his fixed costs while giving him access to a wide range of specialist knowledge.

Using external experts in a training environment has always been associated with some degree of controversy. Those against it argue that the organisation is vulnerable to the availability of individuals who are not fully committed to the institution's success. On the other hand if the experts are on the staff then they are guaranteed to be there when required.

Hall made a great success of this external staffing model. His successor largely followed it, but not entirely, as by the 1960s the College was expanding and reducing its reliance on syndicates and thus needed a greater set of intellectual skills. However the College in later years continued to develop external academic staffing or outsourcing to the point where it was virtually an art form.

2.3. The selection of course participants

It is important to note that the courses at the College were not open to the public. In order to be offered a place an individual had to be nominated by his or her employer and as already stated it was the clear intention that only high potential individuals who had already achieved a significant level of success in their organisations should be so nominated. In addition before an individual's place was confirmed he or she had to be interviewed by an acceptance panel at the College.

In fact the 1960 College Handbook states that "admission to the College is by competitive interview"! This effectively meant that the College was

---

[19] There were obviously those who argued that activities in the Thames Valley were strategic to the war effort and therefore a potential target for the Luftwaffe. On the other hand children were sent from London to the Thames Valley in order to avoid the blitz.

in the business of talent spotting as much as anything else and those who were admitted to a course were being endorsed by both their employer and by the College. Because of this it did not take long for the word to get out that if someone had been to a management development course at the College they were marked for "greater things" - as already mentioned they were potential 'captains of industry'. Thus there was some debate in the press as to whether the College course was responsible for some individuals' rapid promotion to senior management, but this was of little consequence.

Course participants were always selected with a view to obtaining well balanced syndicate groups with the appropriate level of diversity. In order to optimise this process the College was eventually to embark on a major research study together with Belbin, which extended over many years and which led to a high degree of visibility for the institution.

2.4.   Course No. 1 March 31 1948

After some delays[20] the first course was launched on March 31 1948. Greenlands was not quite in the state that Hall wanted it and he is on record as having said that the course members would recognise that there was still some post-war austerity in the system and therefore they would not expect all the arrangements to be perfect. The shortages experienced at that time was epitomised by the fact that the joining instructions sent out to the course members reminded them to lodge their ration books with the reception at the College on arrival. Furthermore the note which is reproduced here concerning the College Handbook which was sent out by the Registrar to course members demonstrates some of the challenges the College faced in 1948. It was a very difficult time indeed to be launching a new venture such as the Administrative Staff College.

In every sense Course 1 was a great success and in support of this proposition Harry Slater quotes a course member as saying, "What does one remember? First must surely be the impact of the whole lovely setting of Greenlands and the immediate warmth of welcome from Noel Hall and his able and enthusiastic team. It seemed that everything, whether to do with the course itself, or our comfort and well-being, had been predicted to the last detail".

---

[20] The first Course began one year later than was originally hoped due to the preparation work especially that required to deal with the poor condition of the building.

Staff

Principal:

Noel F. Hall, M.A.

Administrative Assistant: Miss Dean Richardson, M.B.E.
Registrar: S.P. Kipling, B.SC.

Director of Studies:

D.B. Hoseason, M.I.MECH., M.I.E.E.

Assisted by the following directing staff

R.W. Bell LL.M
*H.A. Bullough
Raymond Parmenter, M.A.
R.A.L. Pears ascertain
L. Wollison

Research Assistant: J.A. Spencer M.A.

Librarian: J.H. Williams, B.A., F.I.A.

Bursar: J.H.N. Lawson, M.A.

Stewardess: Miss I.E. Probyn Franck

*On short service leave

Exhibit 2: An extract from a College pamphlet describing the Faculty employed at Greenlands for the opening Course at the College.

On top of everything else members of Course 1 were treated during the third week to a visit from the Prime Minister, Mr Clement Attlee, who in a rather informal way indicated his approval of the College. It was recorded that this rather unpretentious man (despite the fact that he was

Prime Minister of the United Kingdom of Great Britain and Ireland) made a really distinct impact on all those present when he addressed one of the lecture sessions during Course 1.

There is no doubt that the structure and the content of the course suited the audience at which it was aimed and the participants left the College on a cloud of enthusiasm for the opportunity they had been given. It would have been after all the first time any of the course members had received any form of management education or training and so they were being introduced to completely new world knowledge directly applicable to their professional functions. In addition it would have been the first time that they had the privilege of spending 12 weeks in an "agreeable Thames-side country house" and according to a written comment made by one of them they had been in an environment where they had had their comfort and wellbeing "predicted to the last detail".

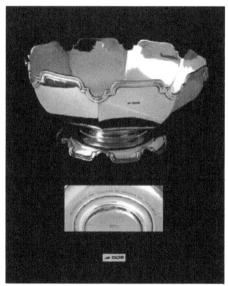

4. A sterling silver bowl bought by grateful members of a course and given to the College as a memento.

Hall and his colleagues had got it right and at the end of Course 1 the College released 45 enthusiastic standard bearers back into their firms who would willingly sell what became known as the Henley experience. Before long there was a waiting list to obtain a place on a College course. Before Hall retired the period required to wait for admission to a College course had become a remarkable two years.

Additional courses were scheduled for June and October 1948.

At the end of 1948 it was universally agreed that the three courses conducted that year[21] had been a great success. However it was also clear that the College had not produced a sensible budget. The operating income derived from the fees had been nowhere near enough and even when the covenanted appeal money

---

[21] It seems that there were only two courses planned originally but with the surprising level of demand the College decided to squeeze a third course into the year.

was added there was still a deficit. The College was financially saved by the fact that it had obtained £10,000 insurance money on the death of Viscount Hambleden which could be used for operating expenses. This of course contrasts with the often expressed belief that the insurance money was used to purchase Greenlands.

2.5.   Other important issues

It did not take long for the news of the success of the Administrative Staff College to spread internationally and within a short period of time there were requests for the College to provide assistance in establishing similar organisations in Australia (Mount Eliza), India (Hyderabad) and Pakistan (Lahore). Interest was also shown by such countries as Ghana, New Zealand and the Philippines. A number of senior members of the faculty visited these other centres and made major contributions to setting up Administrative Staff Colleges there. A comment made by Noel Hall in the Journal of the Greenlands Association[22] is quite instructive regarding how much effort was given to helping those abroad. In addressing the issue of a forthcoming spring cleaning at the College during the summer months Hall remarks:-

> *This is in preparation for a remarkable event that will take place during the last 10 days of September this year when for the first time for several years all the permanent staff of the College will be at Greenlands together.*

Hall goes on to list the various countries where senior members of the College had been working in the previous months or years. It is an impressive list indeed.

This was of course of considerable value to the College which continued to receive nominations from these countries of those who wished to attend the original course at the "mother" College. Henley actually continued to receive a substantial amount of support from course participants from Commonwealth countries right into the 1990s.

2.6.   Steady demand

According to The Times newspaper, by 1950 the demand for places on the courses was such that it was necessary to decline the applications of some of the bigger firms, who had already sent several people on the

---

[22] Journal of the Greenlands Association, Volume 1, No 3, Spring 1958.

courses, in order to make room for individuals from smaller organisations. There was also the question of whether it was proper to reserve places for overseas applicants. One of the issues which exercised the minds of those who were admitting individuals to the College's courses was the question of the balance of individuals. As cross fertilisation by assembling groups of people with different backgrounds was a cornerstone of the philosophy of the College it was important that they selected the right number of people from different industries, professions and activities so that they were well represented in all the different syndicate groups. The College was concerned that they had only managed after several years to attract one trade union employee to attend a course. It was probably over-optimistic that any of the trade unions would want to send an employee to an educational event such as that provided by the College. There was also some disappointment that so few women had attended but the lack of women being nominated for a course really only reflected the fact that there were so few women in senior or even potentially senior positions in organisations in the United Kingdom at that time.

2.7.   Staff observers

There was no doubt that the Administrative Staff College had hit a nerve in the organisational physiology of the nation, as well as that of other countries in different parts of the world. What was happening was so novel that organisations wanted to learn about how syndicate groups actually worked and the College thus created a special class of participant which was called a Staff Observer. A Staff Observer could attend the sessions at the College but would not participate. Such a person did not need to be a high potential senior executive in waiting. They did have to pay the fees.

2.8.   Development and expansion

It had been the intention that there should be 60 members on each Course but due to residential accommodation issues the College had only been able to take about 45. It now wanted to be able to increase the number to 60 and sustain that on a regular basis. Thus the question was how the facilities at Greenlands could be expanded to accommodate more course members. Extra bedrooms were built in what became known as Engine House. Of course this required additional funding which had to be found and this put additional financial pressure on the College.

2.9. The follow-on events

The College course had two distinct effects. The first of these was the high demand for places. The second was that having tasted management education and realising at least to some extent just how vast the subject is and the benefits which could be obtained by knowing more about this subject, course members wanted more. Therefore a number of short follow-on events were developed. The first of these was the weekend refresher course which was arranged by the College for a modest fee. In time this became more substantial and developed into a more general review of management, and short courses were offered to course members 18 months after they had finished their original experience.

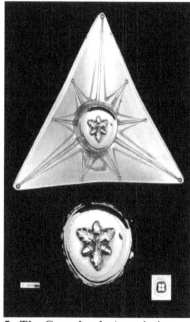

5. The Greenlands Association produced a special sterling silver piece in recognition of the success of the first 10 years of the College. The College has a substantial collection of such gifts offered by grateful Course members.

In 1953 a conference was held to which members of the first 15 courses or sessions (as the College called them) were invited. In general, the conference felt that the College courses were well structured and that the delivery of the events met and exceeded their expectations. However they did ask for some changes which related to changing the work balance between syndicate group work and presentations from members of staff. The College had been aware of the fact that although the syndicate approach was popular with course members there had been some criticism of the fact that not enough formal presentations by faculty were scheduled. In particular the College was asked to provide lectures and exercises relating to the financial aspects of organisations.

It is particularly noteworthy that Hall did not attempt to further expand the range of courses offered by the College. The College's mission was to provide education for general management and this meant that there was no room for specialist training. Also the syndicate method was deeply embedded in the culture of the

College and this approach was not effective in anything other than management education at the highest level.

Over the 12 week residential course a degree of fellowship was established among the participants and this initially led to reunion events and then, 10 years later, to the establishment of the alumni group which was called the Greenlands Association. This was launched at a dinner at Grosvenor House in London in 1956 and nine regional groups were established with one group being in Scotland and one in Wales. The Greenlands Association remained active until recently.

2.10. The Principal resigns

After 15 years service as the leader of the College the Principal was offered the post of Master of Brasenose College at Oxford and decided to take up this position. Hall was 58 years of age at this time.

The search for a new Principal identified Mr JP Martin-Bates, a leading member of the management consulting community, as a replacement and he took up office in August 1961.

2.11. An assessment of the first 15 years

An assessment of the College in the first 15 years of its operation results in a verdict of substantial overall success. It is clear that the initial work of the Court of Governors under Mr Geoffrey Heyworth and the activities of the Principal Mr Noel Hall put the College on the radar of a substantial number of influential individuals and important organisations in the United Kingdom and abroad. It was their particular efforts that ensured the high level of interest in the College's activities. An indication of the national interest in the College is the fact that Prince Philip the Duke of Edinburgh visited.

 Hall and his Director of Studies and their colleagues produced interesting courses and the news of the value of these spread rapidly by word of mouth and by appropriate mentions in the press. The demand for places on the course was so strong that it must have come as a pleasant surprise and have been gratifying to all concerned. The College had been able to create what some would refer to as the myth of the marked man, by which is implied that if a person was nominated for the course and completed it, he or she was going to be going places and would soon be taking up a significant position in senior management. Having this mindset was especially useful to the College because if an individual had been identified for senior management, and their organisation had funded his or her management development at the College, it would not be in his or her interest to be critical of the course.

Noel Hall had a knighthood conferred upon him in 1957, which was no doubt pleasing to him personally, and it also recognised the importance of the work which he had done at the College. Heyworth was elevated to the peerage and became Lord Heyworth of Oxton. There is no suggestion that this peerage happened as a result of his association with the College but it probably did not do him any harm to be seen as a promoter of management education throughout the United Kingdom.

Sir Noel received another significant accolade in that he was invited to be the First Ford Distinguished Visiting Professor at New York University in 1958 and to mark this occasion he was presented with a medal. While in New York he gave a series of three important public lectures in which he outlined his philosophy towards management education. His presence at the University in New York was indicative of his growing international reputation and also the growing realisation of how important the College's programmes had become.

On the downside it is fair to say that the early executives of the College do not appear to have fully understood the finances required to ensure its successful operation. They underestimated the costs of developing Greenlands to a satisfactory level. The location of the College was excellent and the old house had much potential, but it required a considerable amount of renovation and refurbishing. The appeal, which was for an income of £45,000 per annum, was probably much less than what it should have been. In addition they appear to have misjudged the actual operating costs. It had been the intention of the College to fund the operating costs out of a combination of the annual fee income and part of the covenanted subscription, but it transpired that this was difficult to do. The original fee of £150 was clearly too low. It is probable that twice that fee would have been acceptable to the majority of the organisations who were sending individuals to the College and after all the College had the £10,000 bursary fund supplied by the Nuffield Foundation for those few organisations who were not able to afford to sponsor their people. There is often a misunderstanding with regard to not-for-profit organisations. Not-for-profit organisations need to have a clear plan as to how they will fund the capital expenditure and that if this cannot be done out of endowments or gifts or other similar sources then it is necessary to fund capital expenditure out of surpluses. It is interesting that the financial difficulties which the College experienced in those early days remained a feature of the operation of the College for quite some time.

Finally it is probably worth pointing out that Sir Noel Hall's appointment as Master of Brasenose College was the final indicator of his success at the Administrative Staff College at Henley-on-Thames. Being a Master of an Oxford College is probably as great an accolade as can be bestowed on anyone in academe.

Chapter 3

JP Martin-Bates

3.1. Phase Two in the development of the College

In August 1961 Mr James Patrick Martin-Bates accepted the position of Principal of the Administrative Staff College. It is hard to imagine that he knew just how much of a tiger he had grabbed by the tail. Hall had made a great start of creating a significant management education institution in the United Kingdom but there were plenty of issues which were yet to be resolved and it was certainly not an easy job that Martin-Bates had taken on.

JP Martin-Bates, as he is always referred to in College papers[23], did not quite have the academic credentials which Noel Hall was able to bring to the College. Educated at Worcester College in Oxford, Martin-Bates had spent five years in industry before moving into management consultancy at which he was successful, becoming the managing director of Production Engineering Consultants from 1953 until his departure for Henley in 1961. When he decided to retire from the College he continued with an active career. In his consultancy work he had been involved in management education and so he saw the move to the College as a natural extension of that interest. It appears that Martin-Bates, being somewhat dapper and clearly a man of business, more closely complied with Lord Heyworth's image of what a Principal of the Administrative Staff College should be than his predecessor. That is not to say that Martin-Bates and Heyworth saw eye-to-eye on everything.

On arrival at the College Martin-Bates was faced with the interesting challenge of what to do about the two-year waiting list of nominees to be allocated a place on a College course. To some a two-year waiting list or a two-year order book might sound like a fabulous gift. However there is

---

[23] The invitation to Martin-Bates's memorial service suggests that he was known to his friends as Martin.

a downside to having this type of pent-up demand and an inability to satisfy it. The two-year waiting list meant that others would exercise their minds as to ways in which the demand might be satisfied. It is also important to say that by 1961 it had become apparent that management education should be available on a large scale, not only to mid-career individuals but also to those who were setting out on careers which had the potential to lead eventually to management positions. Peter Drucker had been teaching management at the University of New York since 1950 and he also had his seminal book The Practice of Management published in that year. This meant that the subject of management was one which could be or in fact should be addressed at universities, colleges and other institutions of higher or further education. This was to raise its head in a big way in the next few years.

Martin-Bates took on the challenge of proposing a major expansion in the facilities of the College. He actually proposed that a so-called "Second College" be constructed. The idea was simple enough as he did not wish to find another site. What he proposed was to build another set of College facilities on the other side of the Henley-Marlow Road where the College had plenty of open space. There was some merit in this suggestion but the founding fathers were fundamentally conservative and risk avoiders. In the end this proposal was declined by the Court of Governors. On reflection this may well have been the correct decision as splitting the College in this way might have led to an attitude of the College near the river being the A College and the College on the other side of the road being the B College. Also it is pretty obvious that the Court of Governors did not want to undertake the type of fundraising appeal which would have been required to put together the funds needed for such a large development. In reality, the fees which were now at £350 per course were still far too low. So the College lived with its long waiting list which was eventually to spur others on to take competitive positions in the market.

3.2. Changes in society

Superficially the 1960s was famous for its miniskirts, the Beatles, young men's long hair and of course rock 'n' roll. But it was also a time of rethinking of our society and the opportunities for advancement which it offered people. Opportunities and advancement are highly correlated with education and thus the Government initiated two commissions, namely the Robbins Report[24] and the Franks Commission[25] to look into how education should be developed in the United Kingdom. The reports which resulted from the work of both these commissions affected the College. But it was the Franks Commission that had the most impact on the future of management education. Martin-Bates had been called to offer advice to the commission and he had supported the idea that the United Kingdom should develop business schools. Martin-Bates did not see business schools as being directly competitive with the College. To his mind business schools would be delivering management education to young individuals either in the form of undergraduate degrees or as postgraduates in their 20s. He saw the College as being firmly entrenched in the mid-career development phase which addressed individuals in their mid to late 30s and perhaps even into their early 40s.

The Franks Commission eventually recommended that two business schools be established, one of which was to be in London and the other in Manchester. It is surprising that Martin-Bates did not realise that these institutions would soon turn their attention to the fertile market which was composed of mid-career individuals wanting to enhance their knowledge of management. From the establishment of the London and the Manchester Business Schools in 1966 the Administrative Staff College was sitting on a proverbial time bomb.

The 1960s saw a significant change with respect to the type of person who was attending the College. In 1948 the Director of Studies had commented that many of the managers who would attend the College might have had only minimal secondary education. By the mid-1960s half of the course members had degrees and it became necessary for the Course content to reflect that it had to address the concerns of a much more educated member. An article in The Financial Times on August 23

---

[24] The Robbins Report on Higher Education, chaired by Lord Robbins was commissioned in 1961 by the British government. It was accepted and published by the Government on 24 October 1963. The report recommended an immediate expansion of universities. It suggested that university places "should be available to all who were qualified for them by ability and attainment" (the so-called Robbins principle). It argued that a university was essential to any balanced society and not merely to produce specialists. It also proposed that there should be a balance between research and teaching which should not be regarded as entirely separate activities.

[25] The Franks Commission reported in 1966 more directly addressed the issue of management education with a proposal for the urgent creating of two business schools to service demand in the United Kingdom in London and Manchester. It is the Franks Commission report which is always referred to when discussing the fate of the Administrative Staff College.

1967[26] pointed out that the College did not have a computer and it goes on to say:-

One can make too much of this, but it demonstrates that the staff at Greenland's [sic] have a lot of rethinking still to do. In the face of the growing popularity of the new business schools, with their short courses for middle management, the pre-emptive place that the College has always had is under constant siege, and the danger is that the more Henley changes to meet the challenge, the more it will become like its competitors (if that is the word for them).

The Financial Times writer overestimated the use of computers in the United Kingdom at that time but nonetheless the point he made is valid and the College was about to have to work hard to keep its competitive advantage alive and well. One of the issues was the fact that the term business school was new and it generated an increased level of interest in the idea of management education. Nonetheless the College stayed with the name Administrative Staff College for some years to come.

3.3. The camouflage is removed

It was only in 1964 that the College's pristine white visage was established when money became available to improve the appearance of the buildings.

3.4. The scope of the job of Principal

Martin-Bates travelled the world helping the establishment of Staff Colleges in a number of different countries. In his "newsletter from the Principal" published in the Journal of the Greenlands Association he describes his travels abroad in the autumn edition of 1967:-

The College's work in overseas countries is continuing, and new ground is being broken. Colleges are already established in Australia, India, Pakistan and the Philippines, but we have recently been engaged in both Africa and Iran, and there are other countries with whom we are having discussions at the moment. Financial help from the Ford Foundation in America, from the Ministry

---

[26] *Henley gets tough* by Willem Van Der Eyken, The Financial Times on August 23 1967.

of Overseas Development and from the Leverhulme Trust[27] has been provided for this work. There has been a notable increase in the number of visitors from abroad, many of them representing responsible organisations who wish to set up training establishments on Staff College lines.

This overseas work took Martin-Bates away from the College for extended periods of time during which the College was run quite effectively by the Deputy Principal.

It is not clear from the evidence available if Martin-Bates and the other senior College executives who travelled abroad were paid directly for their time abroad but it does seem that these overseas activities were of direct benefit in making the world aware of the College and this led to increases in overseas course members. The flow of overseas individuals attending courses persisted beyond Martin-Bates right up to the end of the following Principals' terms of office. Martin-Bates was certainly working for the long-term future of the College.

3.5. Expanding the research department

Martin-Bates was able to report that the Research Department was expanded to five people and in addition other members of staff who had been drawn into development and research projects were also participating in the activities of this enlarged group. There had previously been a clear distinction between teaching and research staff and this had now been relaxed. The grant they had received from the Foundation for Management Education had been most useful in helping to develop this new activity. In addition to research projects this group had now commenced the publishing of books and other documents which would be made available to course members and students at other universities. Martin-Bates was now of the view that the College was ready to receive visiting researchers who could come to Greenlands with confidence to pursue their research interests.

---

[27] The Leverhulme Trust is a foundation based in London established in 1925 under the will of William Lever, 1st Viscount Leverhulme to support "scholarships for the purposes of research and education."

3.6.   Working with the Tavistock Institute

In 1966 Martin-Bates initiated a review of the course by the Tavistock Institute which took all of three years. This review made a detailed examination of the College's approach to management education and development and this included both how the course was conducted as well as the issues addressed during the 12 week period. It was quite possible for the College to undertake such a review itself but it was decided to employ an outside professional organisation because the College wanted to have access to the personal opinions of former course members and it was felt they could not obtain objective opinions using their own staff. Long complex questionnaires were used as well as detailed personal interviews. It was said that 300 variables resulted from the questionnaire data. Some preliminary findings of the Tavistock research were reported in the Journal of the Greenlands Association volume 3 number 5 Spring 1969 as follows:-

> *The replies revealed an emphasis upon the value of informal contacts with other members, directing staff and visitors to syndicates. As a result of these interactions, members came to see themselves, their enterprise and their fellows more objectively, at the same time developing personally and increasing in self-esteem. By way of modification to existing methods many of the members would have liked the staff to have exercised more direct leadership and have demonstrated their own competence as teachers more frequently, especially in the field of computers, economics, and quantitative analysis. Other members expressed a wish for more help in self appraisal by means of private seminars and counselling.*

The full findings of the review were long and complicated. Some saw the report as being highly critical of the College and what they were trying to do. There is no doubt that the Tavistock Institute were not as supportive of the syndicate method as the College would have liked. Both Hall and Martin-Bates put a lot of faith in syndicates and although the latter now understood it was necessary to move at least to some extent to more traditional methods of instruction, this was done with a degree of sadness. The Tavistock exercise resulted in the Course being restructured with less syndicate work and more formal teaching sessions. There was also an introduction of more technical topics and at the same time the course was reduced to 9 weeks. Another result of this review was that the College employed more experts of its own and relied less on visitors to address specialist subjects. It was certainly indicative of Martin-Bates that he was not in any way apprehensive about bringing in experts to review the work that was going on in order that it might be improved.

3.7. Something for older managers

Another spin-off of the reviews which took place at this time was the introduction of the General Management Appreciation Course which was intended for older managers who would have been above the age limit set for the original course. The demand for this came from the younger potentially top managers who had completed the main College event and who wanted their superiors to be exposed to the same sort of ideas they had been. This course was eventually going to be renamed the Senior Course in 1977. It used the same combination of syndicate group work, exercises and lecturers.

Operations research

The offering of operations research courses was a major move for the College away from the founders' original aims of providing management education for those who were likely to join their organisations' senior management team in the near future. This is the first evidence of the fact that the College had realised that there was a greater set of opportunities available if it broadened its focus to include subjects other than general management.

Martin-Bates took an important step away from the College's emphasis on cross-fertilisation. Cross fertilisation relied on the idea of bringing people together from different industries and from the civil or military service for example. At the end of the 60s the insistence on this type of mix of people on a College course began to be eroded with specialist courses being set up for particular organisations. The first of these courses was designed and developed for the Civil Aviation Authority and this was the beginning of a long list of such clients. At the same time Martin-Bates realised that the age of the specialist manager had arrived and the College began to add subject specific courses to its list of offerings. One such early programme offered instruction in operations research topics and addressed the subject of linear programming and queuing theory and this course was open to any manager who was interested in this field.

It was at this time that a computerised business game was introduced into the course. The game required intensive team work which reinforced this dimension of learning opportunity at the College. Research was now conducted into optimal team work which involved Dr Meridith Belbin and this initiative led to a period of collaboration between the College and him. This project started out as a relatively minor activity but developed into a major research study with multiple organisation and training implications for around a decade. Further the ideas introduced by Belbin were directly connected to personality testing and this brought another dimension to the activities of the College. In turn this led to Personal Development and Competencies Research and eventually, largely as a result of the national publicity achieved by this research, the College was awarded a contract to conduct another major research project for the UK Department of Employment together with the Institute of Directors.

There was one other innovation which was introduced by Martin-Bates which should be mentioned and that was the Directing International Operations course which was led by Sir James Lindsay. Lindsay was a seasoned multinational corporation operator having been chairman of Metal Box in India for a number of years; on his return to the United Kingdom he wanted to be involved in disseminating the knowledge he had acquired during that period. This course attracted considerable numbers initially but the College was not able to sustain its popularity as a separate course and as it had a significant overlap with another course the two were combined into one.

3.8. A new academic staffing model

Acquiring appropriate academic staff was always a challenge for the College. Hall had been aware of this from the beginning. As has been discussed in the previous chapter, Hall had kept the team at the College to the bare minimum, supporting these individuals by inviting specialists to the College to fill in the gaps in the knowledge and experience of his inhouse team.

Although Martin-Bates continued with this model he found it necessary to employ directly on a permanent basis some extra staff as he began to respond to the requests which surfaced as a result of the research conducted by the Tavistock team, and also as the College expanded the range of events it was offering. The College was always most careful about the size of the permanent faculty and the level of remuneration which was paid. As will be seen later the College was able to operate on a small number of full-time permanent academics with a much larger group of part-time temporary faculty.

3.9. A new source of funds

When the Franks Commission report was presented the government launched an appeal for funds with which to kick start the new business schools. The College applied for some of this money being distributed by the Foundation for Management Education (FME). In late 1964 the College's application was declined as it was not linked to a university. Although the College was intensely protective of its independence, members of the Court of Governors began to realise that maybe there was an advantage to be had from an association with a university. University funding was not enormously generous, but at this stage the College had to seek out money on a piecemeal basis from appeals and the fees still did not cover the costs.

3.10. The two year waiting list evaporates

To make matters worse, during the latter years of Martin-Bates' term in office the two-year waiting list for the main Course slowly but surely declined. In the end although the demand for places on this event was still strong the waiting list was minimal. The glory days when the College was the only way of obtaining mid-career management education were over.

3.11. A link with a university

At this time it was not altogether clear what a link with a university might mean. University education was generally perceived as being for the young. The traditional education model was that a young person stayed at school until their late teens and obtained university entrance by passing A-level examinations. After this a University was attended, normally for three years, to obtain a bachelors degree which in England was typically an honours degree. This was the full extent to which an individual would be taught about a particular discipline. After the bachelors degree if the individual wished to extend his or her study they would undertake a programme of research which would lead to a Masters degree. Hardly anyone, even those who intended to pursue a career as an academic teacher, continued with a programme of study beyond the Master level i.e. leading to a doctorate.

Thus in the traditional academic hierarchy a Masters degree was only undertaken after a first bachelors degree and was therefore referred to as a postgraduate degree.

However in the late 1960s it became clear that there should be an alternative route to academic education, especially for those who did not have the opportunity to remain at school into their late teenage years. The establishment of the Open University was one reflection of this. Other universities began to allow certain mature individuals who had not completed the traditional route of A-levels and a bachelor's degree to register for a Masters degree which would soon be referred to as taught Masters. The taught Masters degree generally consisted of a series of courses and a short dissertation. This model became popular and it suggested itself to some of the members of the Court of Governors as a way forward to new markets for management education for the Administrative Staff College.

Some might consider it ironical that the taught Masters degree was somehow still considered by many universities to have the same status as the older research Masters, although it could be taken as a first degree and a first degree is generally not considered to be a postgraduate degree.

In the 1960s there was a considerable amount of antipathy towards the taught Masters. Some academics argued that this approach was often too superficial and that graduates with this type of degree did not have a real understanding of the subject they had been studying. The argument was that to obtain a full grasp of all the issues in the discipline it was necessary to spend the undergraduate years exploring the subject in the amount of detail which can only be addressed over a three-year period. Of course there is some truth in this argument, but it is also surprising how much knowledge a highly motivated learner can acquire from a taught Masters.

It would be on the basis of setting up a taught Masters that the College explored a university linkup.

3.12. Funding research

Martin-Bates and the chairman of the then Court of Governors Sir Duncan Oppenheim made another appeal to the FME but to little avail. The College was granted £100,000 over a period of five years to fund research and other staff development activities but there would be no money for any development of the property. The College attempted to balance its books by running an additional general management course that year. In 1965 four courses were offered in order to help alleviate the financial situation. In addition the fees were increased to £650. But these were relatively small sums compared to the funding which the College could access if it was considered by the University Grants Commission (UGC) to be eligible. It really made sense to try to find a way of accessing UGC money.

Despite the increase in the number of courses and the additional income-generating fees, the College still had difficulty in balancing its books. It had become obvious that the College needed to take a really new course of action which would allow it to operate on a level playing field with the other business schools which were now established, and which were likely to open up in the near future. After more than a decade in the job Martin-Bates was due to retire in 1972, when he would be 60 years of age, and a committee was set up to find a successor. The committee had in mind to find an individual who would be able to lead the College into a relationship with a university which would give it a new range of opportunities, but which would not simultaneously destroy the College's independence. This was of course a tall order.

The name of Professor Tom Kempner was mentioned as such an individual. Kempner was not unknown to the College as he had worked there during the early days when Noel Hall was Principal and was photographed as part of a class group. Kempner had been a relatively junior researcher and he had left the College to take up a full academic appointment as a lecturer in the Department of Economics at Sheffield University.

After preliminary discussions it was decided that Kempner was the man the committee was looking for and he was made an offer to join the College, and he became Principal designate until Martin-Bates had retired. It was now a question of finding the right university with whom to establish the association.

3.13. An assessment of the Martin-Bates years

These were truly pioneering days during which the College showed a high degree of success. Not only was there a substantial waiting list for places on College courses, but important people from overseas beat a path to the College door in order to learn about its approach to mid-career management development. It is interesting to reflect on how the original model for the financial operation of the College evolved during the Martin-Bates period. The idea that the fees charged for attendance should be held at a low level is interesting. The College was attracting attendees from the biggest organisations in the land and yet the Court of Governors seemed to feel that it was inappropriate to charge a full cost fee. This may in part be due to the fact that there were no cost accountants among the people who were in charge of running the College. The failure to put the College on a solid financial footing was to haunt it, then and perhaps for years to come.

It is interesting to wonder what might have happened if Martin-Bates's idea of a second College had been accepted. Did the Court of Governors refuse this idea because they knew that doubling the size of the College would have meant greater financial headaches as they would have been losing money at perhaps twice the rate they already were? Or, was the strategy to keep the number of individuals with which the College could cope low so that places on the course had a scarcity value?

Reading Martin-Bates's writings during his principalship it is obvious that he was an intensely committed and active leader of the College. He put a remarkable level of energy into promoting the College in every way he could. He was open to new ideas. He was especially aware of the importance of the Greenlands Association and he made it a feature of his tenure as Principal that he visited the various branches of the Association around the country. But this was not enough to prevent the numbers applying for the courses at the College from declining and it was clear that material changes had to be made to the way the College functioned.

With his retirement coming up in 1972 Martin-Bates really needed to keep the ship on course and all the big challenges of reconstruction and transformation which were beginning to raise their heads as his date of retirement approached would have to be taken care of, by whoever succeeded him in the role of Principal.

There were discussions in the press as to the effectiveness of the management education obtained by attending the College. It was suggested by some commentators that the real skill of the College was talent spotting in that the College decided whom it would accept on its course. Although there was no doubt some truth in this allegation it would be unfair to say that the management education delivered by the College made no contribution to course members' ultimate success in their careers. As mentioned before there had been criticism of the syndicate method and Martin-Bates had taken this to heart so that by the time he left the College, the course had been redesigned and syndicate work was now only one part of a mix of educational delivery methods.

The 11 years during which Martin-Bates was Principal of the College saw the management education environment in the United Kingdom dramatically altered. Whereas Noel Hall had a clear run at the market in 1948, as Martin-Bates's tenure ended the College had to face considerable competition. Furthermore the competition which was being offered by business schools was at least in some part funded by the government through their grants to universities. It had become clear that the College could not carry on operating in the 1970s in the same way it had done over the previous 20 years of its existence without encountering serious financial problems.

Although there was no knighthood offered to James Patrick Martin-Bates, after he retired from the College he continued a distinguished career including being a UN consultant in Iran and becoming the High Sheriff of Buckinghamshire. He was appointed to several other offices of note including being a member of the Council of the University of Buckingham.

Most would agree that Martin-Bates had distinguished himself as a competent Principal of the Administrative Staff College at Henley-on-Thames.

Chapter 4

The Kempner Years

4.1. The long journey to transformation

Whereas Hall got the College going and in so doing pioneered mid-career management education, Kempner transformed this small operation into a global business school by pioneering distance learning for an MBA.

6. Professor Thomas Kempner

When I first arrived at the College in 1988 I was struck by how different the environment was to anywhere I had worked before. Not only was it a beautiful location but there was an especially active buzz about the place. In addition there was an unusually high level of gossip about the institution and some of the key people in it. One of the people about whom there was much said was the Principal, Professor Thomas Kempner. I was told by several people that he had been in office as Principal for more than 30 years. In fact, in 1988 he had been Principal for 16 years. But like a lot of gossip there was some foundation to this misinformation. Thomas Kempner had a long association with the College in that he had originally joined the College in 1954 as a junior research officer and stayed in that post for 5 years before moving on. Thus in 1988, his association with the College would have begun 34 years before, but not as Principal. Another comment often heard was that the Principal made all the important decisions for the institution.

Of course, this was an exaggeration although it did indicate that Kempner had his finger directly on the pulse of all the important events which occurred in the College. He was a hands-on Chief Executive who had successfully led the organisation through the difficult 1970s and the early 1980s and this required a high degree of attention to detail. Furthermore he lived on the grounds of the College and he was fully engaged in making sure the College continued to succeed. There were also comments about Kempner and his ability with money. Kempner's two predecessors, Hall and

Kempner was not a man of great charisma, nor was he especially striking in appearance. Rather he was an individual who exuded a deep sense of competence. It was clear that he commanded respect from all his staff and that he was seen as the person who really understood the needs of the College, and that he knew how to lead it to success. He was a man of determination with the energy to carry it out. There was no question that he was "the-commander-in-chief".

Martin-Bates, had had considerable difficulty in balancing the financial books. They appeared not to have been aware of how essential adequate financial information and control systems were in sustaining a business. Kempner was especially conscious of making sure that an appropriate fee was charged for the College's courses and that costs were controlled. As a result Kempner had put the College on a much firmer financial footing. There was nothing magic about this as it was simply sound business prac-

tice but Kempner was seen as somehow having the Midas touch.

It is difficult to know whether the Court of Governors had any idea of just how radically the new Principal would change the College when they appointed him in 1972. He was to reinvent the College so that it would hardly be recognisable to its founding fathers.

Thomas Kempner had read economics at University College London before taking a junior position as a research officer at the Administrative Staff College at Henley-on-Thames in 1954. From here he was offered a lecturing position in the Department of Economics at Sheffield University where he remained until he took up the post of Professor of Management Studies and Head of School at Bradford University in 1963. At Bradford he founded the University's Management Centre and became its first Director. Before coming to the College, Kempner was a nationally recognised academic with an extensive publication record. His contribution to both management theory and practice was recognised by the British Institute of Management which awarded him the Burnham Medal. He had also been made member of the Council of the Royal Economic Society.

It is one thing to aspire to have a link with a university but it is quite a different matter to establish one. Universities are famously difficult about whom they will have relationships with and how these relationships will operate. Although Martin-Bates was an Oxford graduate, his consultancy career might have made discussions with universities more challenging than it was for Kempner, who was clearly a university man. There were not many universities within easy reach of Henley-on-Thames. It is true that Oxford University was not far away but this long established blue brick institution would not have been expected to want to do business with a relatively young institution. This was especially true for an institution engaged in teaching a then relatively questionable academic subject, i.e. the study of management. The other nearby University of Reading was at the time deeply engaged in its own programmes. In the event, Brunel – the University of West London - showed interest in coming to an arrangement with the College. The new Vice Chancellor at Brunel was interested in developing a capability in the field of business and management and a relationship with Henley was exactly what he required at that time. Brunel University itself had only come into existence in 1966 when it had been granted a Royal Charter. Although it was much less common in the early 1970s for universities to have multiple campuses, Brunel University was situated only 25 miles away, which was not a distance to produce any great problem from the point of view of staff being able to deliver programmes in either or both sites.

The work done by the College since its inauguration in 1948 was well-known in the United Kingdom and therefore an association with such a well-established institution was greeted by Brunel Senate with some enthusiasm. Part of the agreement between the College and the University was that a new Principal would simultaneously be appointed as Professor of Management Studies at Brunel University. He would be co-opted onto the Brunel University Council as would another member of the College's Court of Governors. Kempner was also to be a member of the University Senate. At the same time two members of Brunel University would serve on the College's Court of Governors. It was intended that the College would assist Brunel University in developing new joint courses in management and Brunel would be in a position to recognise new degrees which the College would offer. The agreement with Brunel specifically provided for the College to continue with its post-experience courses which would fall out of the ambit of Brunel University's interest in the College's activities. In this way the College and Brunel became associated institutions while the College retained its autonomy.

As the link with Brunel was established the University Grants Committee (UGC) added funds for another 100 postgraduate students to Brunel's grant to help the new relationship on its way.

It is worth pointing out that not all of the College's staff welcomed the association with Brunel University. Some of the older members of faculty believed that in tying up with the university the College would be selling out on its original principles which were to deliver quality management development to mid-career individuals. They felt that being part of a university would inevitably mean working with younger and less established students and that this would in some way detract from the College's excellent reputation. There was a strong belief in the College that they did not want to become just another business school like the many that were being created as departments in universities in various parts of the United Kingdom. These misgivings were misplaced as the College did not attempt to become active in the undergraduate business school arena, but used the Brunel connection to good effect in developing postgraduate degrees. Of course those who undertook postgraduate degrees at business schools were generally younger and less experienced than the type of individuals at whom the College aimed when it first offered courses in 1948. But this was what was needed in the mid-1970s as the market for mid-career management education had now profoundly changed.

4.2. In the first years of Kempner

In 1973 the College continued business as usual. The General Management course was run three times and the shorter General Management Appreciation course was run twice. The relatively new Directing International Operations event also ran on two separate occasions. The College ran 18 open short courses on a variety of subjects as well as 21 other courses for the Civil Aviation Authority. Although the idea of a group photograph had already been established at Henley since its early days Kempner was an enthusiastic advocate of this practice and a significant number of group photographs were taken over the years of which the following is but one.

At the same time as these events were being conducted plans were being made to enter the Masters degree education business and by October 1973 the College was ready to announce its first joint programme with Brunel – a residential Masters programme which would lead to an MA in business.

4.3. The Kempner team

To become credible in the degree-awarding world it was necessary for the College to expand its team of competent academics. In the early 1970s it was not easy to find individuals who could fill the roles now required at the College.

It is only possible here to describe a small number of the staff who came to work for the College and it is important to emphasise that there are many more that played central roles in the success of the institution.

Kempner attracted to the College a number of individuals with whom he had worked at Bradford University. In general these individuals took on key positions and they were regularly referred to by those who did not commence their academic careers in Bradford as the Bradford Mafia[28].

The first to join the College amongst this group of people was Ray Wild. Kempner recruited Wild to develop and manage the new Masters degree. A distinctly innovative approach was taken which involved modules of instruction, in-service work periods and then a final dissertation. It was an original attempt to combine academic education with hands-on work experience which was attractive to both degree candidates and their employers.

This Masters degree attracted 15 candidates and was launched in May 1974. The number of registrations for this degree grew throughout the 1970s and by the end of that decade it was attracting between 40 and 50 candidates each year. It was also decided that the degree should be re-named and it became an MBA.

Wild was to eventually follow Kempner as the Principal of the College when Kempner retired.

Another member of the former Bradford team was David Birchall who joined the faculty soon after the arrival of Kempner and who was to play a number of significant roles in the College especially with regard to research. In later years he was to be a member of the College's management team and to head up one of the College's two divisions referred to as the Henley Research Centre. This centre was important in attracting funded research to the College. Birchall was regarded as a significant

---

[28] The term Bradford Mafia was unfair as it implies a high degree of coherence and self-serving behaviour, which does not appear to have been present among this group.

scholar and was highly admired by many members of the faculty. He remained at the College until he retired.

Colin Carnall was also a Bradford man who joined the College and was energetic and highly active in the College management over a number of years. Also regarded as an outstanding scholar he concentrated on the management of different types of MBA programmes which evolved over the years. He became a member of the management team which ran the College in later years and being highly ambitious he was generally regarded as a significant contender for the Principalship, to which he was not appointed. Also highly admired by members of the College, Carnall eventually moved on to a Chair at another university.

Keith MacMillan was another senior member of faculty who had a longstanding connection with Kempner. He was a scholar of note as well as having an innovative approach to the design and delivery of management education. He was highly concerned about the faculty's interaction with students. Eventually be became the Deputy Principal and Academic Dean where he played a significant role in the College until he retired. MacMillan played an important role in ensuring that the College was recognised by the appropriate accreditation bodies which were becoming crucial in establishing and maintaining the reputation of the College. As Deputy Principal he made the first contacts with John Madejski and was instrumental in building a relationship which led to an important research centre being established. He was also founder Chairman of the Centre for Board Effectiveness. For a number of years he was the Editor-in-Chief of the Journal of General Management. Some of his friends in the College regarded him as just as important as the Principal to the institution. After he retired he became a part-time member of faculty and continued to work with the College on some projects. He was highly respected by everyone who knew him. In discussing with him the challenges which the College faced during his period in office it was clear that he had an in-depth appreciation of the many issues which the College needed to address if it were to sustain its leading position in the management education market. Keith died young in 2003.

A significant addition to the College in the early Kempner years was Tom Taylor. Taylor was an Oxford graduate who had spent some time at the Inland Revenue Services and who had joined the College as finance and accounting specialist. He had previously attended one of the earlier Courses and he returned to the College where he served the institution for the rest of his working career. Taylor was enthusiastic about understanding and controlling the College's costs. He eventually played a greater role than Financial Director, becoming a Deputy Principal and also being the director of the General Management Programme.

Birchall, Carnall, MacMillan and Tom Taylor were to be become the core of Wild's Management Team when he assumed the role of Principal 18 years after Kempner started.

4.4.   The second Taylor at the College

Another significant appointment made by Kempner in this period was that of Professor Bernard Taylor. Taylor had known Kempner from the early days in Bradford and was invited to take a post at the College.

Taylor's subject was corporate strategy and in the years that followed he developed for himself a significant global reputation in this field. At one point he was recognised as being probably the most visible individual at the College. Among his achievements were the establishment of two important academic journals as well as making a major contribution to the Long Range Planning Society. He was much more interested in academic achievement than acquiring any executive or management role within the College. He remained at the College and played a significant role in its development until he retired. In fact after his formal retirement Taylor continued to play an active role as a part-time contractor to the College.

4.5.   Another distinguished academic

It is important to mention that Sheila Rothwell joined the College in 1979 as the Director of the Centre for Employment Policy Studies. She had already enjoyed a distinguished career, having played important roles on a number of government commissions. Her work in human resource management and the role of women in the workforce was extensively published. Although she played a rather low profile in the College her presence was regarded as important to the College's prestige. She continued to be in demand for government commissions and she published widely. She did not have a PhD and this was said to have been the reason why she was not offered a professorship. There were several male professors who also did not have a doctorate and it was generally believed that this was thought by Sheila to be unfair. Sheila became ill, left the College and died in 1997.

For some time the College did not do well with respect to women academics but eventually it was able to claim success in this respect. Nevertheless the College did employ a number of course or programme directors who were women, some of whom were simultaneously regarded as academics. This twin classification was controversial as many of these programme directors had minimal involvement with teaching or research.

4.6. Research degrees

It was also decided that the College should offer research degrees and in the early years of the relationship with Brunel the College began to admit MPhil and PhD degree candidates. Although the number involved in this activity was small at the outset it grew rapidly and within a few years it was recorded that there were 65 people working towards a research degree at the College. Offering doctorates meant that it was necessary to develop an entirely different approach to management education, with the emphasis having to be placed on finding supervisors who were capable of and prepared to work with researchers to assist them in obtaining their degrees. Although in the 1970s those who supervised doctoral degree candidates did not necessarily need to have a doctoral degree themselves it was important that the supervisor be research active. At this time research had not yet become the significant academic activity which it is today and it was a challenge to find individuals who were capable of the tasks involved in research degree supervision.

It was at about this time that The Henley Centre for Forecasting was created. The College's governors joined the Centre's governing body and Kempner became its Chairman. A couple of years later in 1976 another new venture was launched. This was referred to as the Henley Management Development and Advisory Service (HMDAS). This was set up in order to deliver special in-company tailored courses for corporate clients. The College already had some experience of this activity with the Civil Aviation Authority and it now saw this as a fruitful line of business which was to play a major role in the development of the College and which can be seen as the forerunner of the institution's executive education activities.

A number of other short courses were proposed and successfully conducted during the later years of the 1970s. All of this put pressure on College accommodation and new building programmes had to be funded and new class rooms and bedrooms developed.

Looking at the time line in Appendix One, it is reasonable to suggest that the Kempner years were packed with innovation. The College was no longer an institution whose sole purpose was to deliver opportunities of self-improvement to midcareer managers. The College was rapidly developing into a postgraduate business school, although the Court of Governors still eschewed the use of the name Business School.

In 1981 a formal change of name took place and the Administrative Staff College was renamed Henley – The Management College[29]. This signalled an important break with the past and it was now clear to all concerned that the College was much more than an institution designed to deliver mid-career management education.

Kempner wanted to ensure that the College kept abreast of the latest technology developments and an arrangement was made with IBM that a number of IBM-PCs were supplied to the College and one PC was placed in every syndicate room. In fact these computers were not used to any great extent but they remained in these rooms for many years. On one occasion a curious participant asked me if the College was engaged in running a technology museum as a side line. This was said rather sarcastically. In the end these old personal computers were removed.

4.7. The distance learning MBA

Because of the amount of publicity which has been given to e-learning in the past 10 years it is sometimes forgotten that learning at a distance is a very old tradition indeed. Looking back many years we find the well-established idea of home learning from books studied many miles away from any human authorities on the subject learned. Sir Isaac Pitman was offering courses as early as 1840. The University of London had correspondence courses by 1858. By 1873 the University of South Africa was established which was for many years one of the largest correspondence universities in the world. These institutions offered study programmes which involved individuals sending assignments by post which were evaluated and returned in the same way. Perhaps it was the Open University with its ability to produce high quality video that made distance learning really attractive. In any event, during the third quarter of the 20th century there was a realisation that the demand for education was much greater than could ever be delivered through normal channels of direct teacher-student interaction. Distance learning at the College was about to become very important indeed.

---

[29] The new name of the College, Henley-The Management College, was a rather pretentious way of differentiating the institution from the other business schools which were at this stage being created at a large number of universities. The Court of Governors wanted to emphasise the point that the college was not just another business school.

In 1982 the Brunel Senate approved the idea of using distance learning as one of its means of delivering education. This was the green light for Henley to put a substantial amount of energy into creating a distance learning MBA.

Talking to those who were involved in this exercise one gets the distinct feeling of the excitement it generated. The College felt that this degree had to be developed quickly so that it would be one of the first movers in the marketplace. Material which had been used on the currently offered MBA programme had to be redeveloped. A substantial investment had to be made into the production of short videos to support the paper based teaching materials. It was suggested that the College did not have the resources to do all of this on its own and for this reason a new separate organisation was formed. This was Henley Distance Learning (HDL) Limited. The College was able to fund some of the capital needed for this new company and became an important shareholder in this business. But HDL needed additional funding from outside and thus new shareholders were found.

The Henley Distance Learning MBA was eventually launched in 1985 and it satisfied a substantial need which the College was able to convert into a healthy demand. Within a couple of years there were over 2,000 registrations on this programme. Such a large programme required additional staff, both academic and administrators. Many specialist academics were required, but they were not needed on a full-time basis and thus the College expanded its already substantial pool of external tutors who were available to guide distance learning students through the material, as well as mark assignments and examinations.

Up to this point the College had attracted a number of overseas students mainly from India and other Commonwealth countries. These students had made important contributions to the groups they had joined. The numbers involved were usually between 12 and 20 a year. This allowed the College to state that it was international. With the marketing of the distance learning MBA Henley became a global institution with students participating in this programme from countries all around the world. It was because of this distance learning programme that the College was able to claim on its 50th anniversary that it was working with 10,000 students from some 80 different countries.

Each distance learning student had to be supplied with a comprehensive work pack which consisted of a variety of notes and other reading materials including academic papers, textbooks, videos, exercises and self tests.

The physical operation to create and compile these packs was quite substantial. In addition to the learning materials the College provided some face-to-face support in the form of occasional seminars. However these seminars were not available in all locations or necessarily scheduled at regular periods. Over the years when it was known that a particular person was travelling to a location on other business he or she was invited by the College to deliver a seminar to support the distant learning MBA in some far distant corner of the world.

By 1988 when I joined the College as a doctoral degree candidate it was able to declare that it had about 7,500 active MBA degree candidates. By any standards this was an extraordinarily large body of students and I always wondered how the College was able to cope with such a large number. It was said that at that time there were more than 100 administrators employed by the College to handle this. It is not known what the information systems infrastructure was nor the IT capability of the College at that time.

4.8.   Reactions to the Distance Learning MBA

Not everyone in the College considered the distance learning MBA to be the salvation of the institution. There were two groups of people who had reservations. The first group consisted of individuals who had worked at the College for many years and who believed that the College's raison d'être was to provide mid-career management education of the sort invented by Hall and refined by Martin-Bates. As far as they were concerned the College should have persisted with this market and overcome the competitive pressures which had been generated by the likes of London and Manchester Business Schools.

The second group consisted of academics who were not convinced that an MBA should or even could be delivered by means of distance learning. There were those in the College who saw distance learning as being nothing more than a euphemism for correspondence learning which they viewed as distinctly inferior to face-to-face learning. It may well be true that there was and still is a large need in society to help individuals acquire knowledge who do not have easy physical access and are thus not able to attend an institution in person. There was also another argument concerning the provenance of the distance learning MBA which will be discussed below.

The crux of the matter is that there is no universally accepted definition of what constitutes an MBA and how it should differ from an MA or an

MSc in business studies. Some academics argued that an MBA is simply a consumer choice in the sense that a university or a business school names its degrees in terms of what is acceptable to the market. Others argue that there should be a more rational and pedagogical underpinning in the way in which degrees are named. The original model of the MBA involved pedagogical processes which are similar to those employed by Hall in his construction of the original Administrative Staff College 12 week residential course. The original idea of an MBA consisted of a considerable amount of group work with degree candidates learning from one another as well as reflecting on their own work experience to date[30]. It is difficult to deliver this type of experience through a distance programme of study. Of course the contrary view is that an MBA, an MA and MSc are simply different names for a taught Masters which in the business studies environment could have the same syllabus and modus operandi. That seemed to be the dominant view at the College.

There was no public debate among the staff of the College about the appropriateness of the distance learning MBA.

4.9. Certificate, diploma and degree progression

One of the ways in which the College made its distance learning MBA attractive to a large number of prospective students was through a multi-staged enrolment route. Whereas many business schools required Masters degree candidates to have an honours degree or perhaps even a simple bachelors degree the College allowed non-graduates to register for a certificate in management. On successful completion of the certificate an individual could then register for a diploma and in turn when this was completed he or she would then be in a position to undertake the Masters degree. This approach opened up a steady route of progress through the academic maze and it made Henley much more accessible than many other business schools at the time. Thus by the time the College reached its 50th anniversary the distance learning MBA programme was one of the biggest in the world and it dominated the fortune of the College.

4.10. Research degrees

It had been a challenge for the College to establish an active research degree programme. As mentioned earlier it was and still is difficult to find supervisors and it is also difficult to guide would-be research degree can-

---

[30] See An MBA Voyage of Discovery, Deep Down the Rabbit Hole, by Dan Remenyi 2014.

didates through the process of the degrees within a reasonable period of time. Research degree are famous for non-completion or for being extended over extraordinarily lengthy periods. In 1988 it was decided to recruit Professor Arthur Money as the new director of doctoral research. When he first took over this role the research degree programme was poorly funded and it took some years and a large amount of innovative thinking to correct this situation. Money became one of the most respected professors at the College.

The major research degree innovation which took place was the establishment and the launch of a Doctor of Business Administration (DBA) degree. This was an instant success and as will be mentioned later it brought much kudos to the College.

4.11. Other College initiatives

The Kempner years saw numerous short courses, seminars and conferences being offered by the College. Kempner understood that the more activity the College could produce the more it would become a significant element in the education of managers both in the United Kingdom and in the broader global context. In this respect Kempner was a very successful Principal.

The list of initiatives which were brought to fruition during the Kempner years is too long to recount fully here, but looking at the brochures produced during this period one cannot but be impressed by the amount of energy and high degree of innovation which the team at the College showed.

There was clearly no reluctance to stray away from the original model developed in the late 1940s.

However there were still challenges to be faced, one of which was the small number of women who were attending the College courses as well as the lack of women members of faculty.

4.12. Accreditation

By the end of the 1980s it had become important for business schools to establish their credibility in the education market place by obtaining accreditation from one or more bodies which monitored the quality of the degree programmes being offered. In the end the College was to obtain triple accreditation but the first formal accreditation came through in 1990 from AMBA, the Association of MBAs.

4.13. The Kempner management style and structure

During the Kempner years the College worked effectively with the original management development courses, the now well-established short courses and the new MBAs. However, as a doctoral degree candidate at that time it was not obvious to me how the College actually functioned. There did not appear to be any subject groupings as one would normally expect to find in a business school. Thus, although in my subject of Information Systems Management there were four individual faculty members delivering courses on this topic, there did not seem to be any coordination between them. The person who held the title of lead tutor ran some courses and as he was the only PhD in this field, he also supervised me. But he had no influence on what the others lecturers in Information Systems Management were doing. Work allocation on this subject seemed to be controlled by administrators who made the decisions which would normally be in the hands of the head of a subject department.

Another interesting aspect of the College was the role performed by professors. At the College a professor did not seem to be a leader in a subject area. Professors seemed to be highly involved in administrative and management issues rather than academic ones. Of course being so new to the College I was not aware of the fact that there were university appointed professors who received their title from the University of Brunel and there were College professors who received their title through a professorial appointments board set up by the Principal, Professor Kempner. This board was independent, originally chaired by Professor Asa Lord Briggs, and thus a professorial title was not in the direct gift of the Principal.

A conversation took place one day which illustrated for me the complexity of the relationships among the staff of the College during this period. Over lunch a discussion turned to the question, "How does the College structure actually function?" I wasn't prepared for the first reply from one of the members of the faculty. "I have been here for three years now and I have been trying to answer this question myself. What I have come up with is the fact that we have substantial workloads. We have a material amount of work related to MBA students, full-time, part-time and executive MBAs. We have periods of extraordinarily intensive work related to the executive programmes and then we have some PhD students. In addition to this there is the updating of all the materials related to the distance learning MBA. There are also occasional assignments which are handed down from on high. And this work is allocated by administrators who have relatively little knowledge or interest in the subject matter. The College is a strange place for academics indeed."

Sitting at our table was a visiting professor from overseas who felt that he wanted to make a contribution to this discussion. "You know", he said, "Universities are managed for the honour and glory of the senior professors. All other members of faculty are effectively bit players. It does not matter where in the world you are, the policy of a university is driven by what the senior team regards being in their best interests. And by the way this does not vary much from one university to another or one business school to another. The other academics are the foot soldiers and as you know, although foot soldiers are essential, the system is not designed to be in the interest of low level workers such as lecturers."

The conversation was then expanded by another faculty member who had been at the College considerably longer than the rest of us. He was now in semi-retirement having worked at the College for several decades. "What makes the College particularly interesting is the fact that it is managed by means of the medieval court approach. The Principal is king, of course and he appoints the barons. The barons are powerful heads of sections and as in a mediaeval court the barons are effectively in competition with each other. Thus barons row amongst themselves and occasionally they even row with the king but they are relatively easily put in their place. A baron in the College does not have an academic function. In fact barons are essentially anti-academic seeing their function much more in terms of managing the institution."

This was the first time I had heard of the mediaeval court approach to management and I wondered how good a metaphor it actually was. What of course made it a compelling way of understanding the College was that there was no faculty structure. There were no subject departments or schools. There was the Principal, a small number of heads of sections and then the academics supported by administrators.

"It is interesting to note," continued our long experienced contributor, "the balance between academic staff and administrators. There are probably 30 full-time members of faculty although there is some debate about that number. As distance learning is administratively intensive there are perhaps 200 members of the team required to manage the thousands of MBA students. Of course there is a substantial group of part-time academics; maybe more than the full-time academics and administrators together. Sometimes the question of who is academic and who is administration raises its head. Although this shouldn't be a problem it can be difficult to distinguish between people who should be considered to be teaching faculty and administrators. And the part-time faculty directly affect the culture of the College in a number of different ways not all of which are necessarily positive."

Within a relatively short time I was exposed to private opinions on a number of the issues which underpinned the vague notion of dissatisfaction within the College. These ideas were at that time new to me and I wasn't at all sure how much credence to give them. But hearing these views gave me a look inside the bonnet at the engine which powered the College and what was said did resonate with some of my own observations.

The question which triggered this conversation "How does the College structure actually function?" was not answered. The College structure was essentially flat with Kempner being the Head of College and key players in the College reporting directly to him.

The issue of the flat structure is an interesting one. University faculties tend to be divided into departments or schools in terms of disciplines or fields of study. This can be effective in creating a critical mass of interest especially with regard to research. However it also tends to establish intellectual space between the subjects or fields of study. In a business school environment it is argued that the different subjects should be integrated as much as possible in order to reflect the need for joined-up high level strategic thinking within organisations. This was the basis of the thinking behind the Kempner flat structure in the College.

4.14. The 3rd Principal retires

On his retirement in March 1990 Thomas Kempner was made a Professor Emeritus at both the University of Brunel and Henley Management College. He was 60 years of age.

4.15. The Principal's house

Shortly before he vacated the office of Principal, Kempner moved out of the Principal's house, which was then converted into a number of offices for College staff. This provided comfortable workspace for about a dozen members of staff.

4.16. An assessment of the Kempner years

It would be churlish indeed to suggest that the Kempner years were anything other than an outstanding success. The 18 years of Kempner's reign saw the most astonishing flow of innovation both from a pedagogical and an entrepreneurial point of view. Many in the College were going to miss him and he would eventually be spoken of as perhaps the most important Principal the College had had.

Kempner converted the College from a small scale specialist management development institution to a substantial business school. The Court of Governors may not have wanted the College to incorporate the words business school into its name but that did not detract from the reality of the situation. The College was now a private graduate school of business and was highly dependent upon achieving a high number of registrations for its MBA programmes each year, which had become the life blood of the institution. In achieving this Kempner exploded the visibility of the College and moved it from being a United Kingdom brand to being a global or at least potentially global brand. The Henley MBA degree was sought after and the PhD programme was considered a significantly worthwhile degree as well.

During the Kempner years the College had expanded exponentially. There was now a substantial team of academics together with a significant number of administrative staff. The revenue of the institution had rocketed which of course had been essential to sustain the much larger team of people which now worked for the College. Clearly the College had prospered and this accounted for Kemper being regarded as having the Midas touch.

The College's timing in entering the Distance Learning MBA market was exceptional. It was not so much that the College was able to capture a large share of this market but rather that it was a major player in creating this market in the first place. The idea of delivering an MBA all over the world to people who would otherwise have no access to such an educational programme was little less than inspirational. The issue of whether it was appropriate to call this type of study programme an MBA simply did not arise.

Kempner had encouraged a panoply of short courses and in so doing the College had established working relationships with a wide variety of professional institutions.

At this time there was a high degree of vibrancy in the College. The car park was usually chock-a-block. The dining room was abuzz and there was always a feeling of something happening.

Kempner was conscious of the need to have the College known about by as many associations as possible. Thus even before it became a central issue for all important business schools to obtain accreditation he had established some informal links with the European Foundation for Management Development and the Association to Advance Collegiate Schools of Business.

If there was a downside to this period it was that the Principal's management style and the structure of the College could be confusing. It is quite probable that it did not get the best out of some of the people who worked there. But this unusual structure worked in that environment and the results which were required were achieved. However, a flat management structure such as that used by Kempner can sometimes create problems in the future. Also the fact that three senior faculty members of the College had been former colleagues of Kempner at Bradford allowed gossip to suggest that there was a Bradford Mafia in operation.

When it was announced that Kempner was retiring there was a palpable feeling of excitement in the College. The mood of staff seems to suggest that many people were looking forward to a change of regime as some of them thought that a new approach was required to move the College further forward and there was the distinct hope that a new leader would be able to achieve this.

However it needs to be said that despite the success of the College it was never regarded as a mainstream business school. The College emphasised its private charity status and therefore did not see itself as competing directly with the other public university based business schools. This of course was both a strength and a weakness.

Chapter 5

The Wild Years

5.1. Rumours are running Wild

There was only a short period between the announcement that Kempner was retiring and the naming of his successor. During this time there was a sense of excitement driven by an expectation that change would be good for the College, which had now, in some ways, become overexposed to a Principal who had been in post for 18 years. There were those who thought that a new pair of hands on the wheel would be a "good thing". At one point I encountered a few people discussing who was likely to become the next Principal and one of them said, "Rumours are running Wild". At the time this did not mean much to me and the pun had to be explained.

5.2. The College freshens up

In handing over the College to Professor Ray Wild the Court of Governors were giving the College to the safest pair of hands on the block. Wild had been in-volved with the College for years and he knew how it functioned. He was also on the faculty of Brunel in various capacities and thus he was the ideal man to cement this relationship and to develop it further.

7. **Ray Wild was enthusiastically received as the 4th Principal.**

Kempner had put in place most of the thinking that was needed by the College for the 1990s and thus Wild's mission could be interpreted in nautical terms as "steady as she goes". It is important to note that this comment "steady as she goes" does not in any way suggest that Kempner had exhausted all the opportunities for innovation. Business schools live or die by their ability to be innovative and Wild clearly knew this. In the 11 years in which he was Principal he produced a substantial number of variations in the products and services offered by the College.

Wild was tall and slim, and in a way a striking figure. He had some degree of charisma and he was noted for his obvious charm. He had the skill of making one feel by the end of a conversation with him that what you had said had been heard and that its importance was noted. He did not, however, have the clear cut leadership qualities that Kempner had. He made the point that the College was now run by a Management Team and not by "the-commander-in-chief".

Born in Derbyshire, Ray Wild had left school at the age of 14 with four O Level passes. His first job was that of an office boy from which he progressed to becoming a draughtsman. He undertook an apprenticeship and qualified as an engineer before discovering the world of academe. He took two MSc degrees and a PhD at Bradford University, one in engineering and one in management. In 1973 he was recruited by the College and shortly thereafter seconded to Brunel where he obtained a DSc.

Wild's appointment was different from his three predecessors in that Hall and Martin-Bates had been Oxford men and Kempner had obtained his education from the famous, or perhaps at one time regarded as infamous, University College London[31]. Wild did not have a bachelors degree and the degrees he did have were not from what might be regarded as an establishment institution thus he did not have a strong academic pedigree.

The first task undertaken by Wild was to refresh the appearance of the College reception which had become, in the eyes of a number of people, somewhat dowdy. In Kempner's days the porters had the area immediately behind the front door and in a way this function was reminiscent of a porters' lodge in an Oxford college. The porters' facility was banished to the back of the house and the reception was transformed and it took on the appearance of being in a smart resort. This was the first step of much refurbishment and redevelopment in the main buildings which made the College feel modern and much more inviting.

---

[31] University College London (UCL) was the first university in the United Kingdom to open its doors in 1826 to women as well as persons who were not members of the Church of England. Thus Catholics and Jews and other non-Establishment religions could attend this institution. It was referred to as "that Godless institution in Gower Street". UCL is also known for taking care of the remains of Jeremy Bentham, which consists of his bones held together by hinges dressed up in his clothes. UCL also have Bentham's mummified head which "has glass eyeballs, which are quite striking" in their keep.

Another of Wild's early moves was to democratise the Blue Room. The Blue Room, which is situated directly to the right of the front door as one enters the building, had been the Senior Common Room. It was always a busy room when it was time for refreshments or over the lunch period. In the Kempner days the door was always closed. It was never clear to me who was entitled to go in there, although I was certain that I as a PhD candidate[32] was not, unless invited by a senior member of staff. I think I ventured into the old Blue Room twice. Wild opened this up to any member of staff. The immediate effect was that the popularity of the Blue Room decreased significantly. He then regulated the car parks.

Wild abolished waitress service in the dining room which was now converted into a self-service buffet type arrangement. This was well received by everyone concerned. He also ended the tradition of the senior members of the staff serving the junior members at the College's Christmas dinner[33].

During this period a small but well-equipped gymnasium was built in the College grounds.

Whereas Kempner appeared to be somewhat remote from the non-junior members of staff Wild was far more accessible and it was relatively easy to obtain time in Wild's diary to see and talk to him.

5.3. Faculty and administrators

Wild appeared to have a greater understanding for visual representations of the College. Much prettier brochures were produced and more interesting photographs of the College and the staff were produced.

The number of people who worked at the College at that time was not published, but those who claim to know say that during Wild's time the academic complement grew to about 40 while the external lecturers, tutors, markers and other academic support staff grew to 400. The full-time faculty were based at Greenlands while the external staff seldom needed to attend the College, except perhaps to present a lecture or to be present at a meeting. The extensive use of external faculty allowed the College to punch considerably above its academic weight from the point of view of teaching and delivering the product which constituted the distance learn-

---

[32] The College had a special name for PhD students or candidates and that was Research Associate.
[33] A military tradition, I am told.

ing MBA. At the beginning of Wild's administration there were perhaps only three women academics on staff, but by the time he retired the number had grown substantially.

5.4. The new College structure

Taking the view that some grouping of activities within the College and appointing directors to manage these groupings would be a good thing, Wild established two divisions. The first division, which was referred to as the Programmes Division was headed by Colin Carnall who looked after all the different taught events which the College had to offer. This was a very large domain indeed and was directly at the heart of the College's success. The second division was referred to as the Henley Research Centre and this was managed by David Birchall. The activities of the Henley Research Centre may not have been as revenue critical as those of the programmes division, but this function was of substantial importance to the College. It was out of this group that the new DBA degree was to emerge.

5.5. Faculty groupings

As well as these major divisions Wild also established faculty groupings whereby academics with mutual intellectual and teaching interests would meet to discuss the work they were involved with and how it should function. The faculty groups were Finance, Information and Operations, Human Resource Management and Organisational Behaviour, Marketing and Strategy.

5.6. The Deputy Principal

During the Wild period of office the Deputy Principal began to play a more active role than had traditionally been associated with that office. The incumbent was Professor Keith Macmillan who has been described in the previous chapter. He paid a significant role in that he took care of many of the staff issues which arose during this period. Part of his role was to conduct annual appraisals of faculty members, which he did in such a positive way that he was sometimes considered to be a mentor as well as an evaluator of performance. In addition to having the title of Deputy Principal he also played the role of Academic Dean. His friends in the College referred to him as "the best Principal the College never had".

He was particularly well respected by many members of Faculty and there were some who believed that he was the obvious candidate to become the next Principal of the College. In the event he was not appointed to this role and he retired at the same time as Wild but continued to be active part-time in the College. His importance to the College was considerable. Keith MacMillan took ill and died early.

5.7. Royal Charter

On June 28, 1991 the College was granted a Royal Charter and it received the Great Seal. At this point Henley – The Management College was renamed Henley Management College.

There were several reasons why a Royal Charter was important to the College, the first of which was that it signalled its status within the British education hierarchy as being an organisation which had the approval of the government and to some extent the personal approval of the Crown. This was a useful attribute from the point of view of marketing, especially marketing abroad.

The second reason that the Royal Charter was so earnestly sought by the College was that it allowed it to be considered by the Department of Education for government grants in its own right. This meant that it would not need to go through the University of Brunel in order to obtain direct government funding.

By 1991 it was already clear that the University of Brunel was to establish its own business school and this meant that the rather open and informal relationship with the College enjoyed for 20 years would have to change. As was mentioned earlier the College had always been fiercely proud of its independence and it would not have suited it to have become just another part of Brunel University.

5.8. The original Courses

The original Course designed by Hall and modified by Martin-Bates and Kempner had become known as the General Management Course. The course created by Martin-Bates for managers of more mature years and originally referred to as the General Management Appreciation Course was now the Senior Course. During the Kempner years these courses had remained highly attractive to participants and had been a major source of income for the College.

It came as a considerable surprise when the uptake on both these courses effectively ground to a halt. It did not seem clear why this happened and also why it happened so abruptly. The suggestion was that organisations suddenly began to realise that they were unable to allow important managers to absent themselves from their functions for the multiple weeks required to attend these courses. But there were other factors at play in the economy. This period saw substantial de-layering in organisations and many of the middle-manager roles from which the College had received support were taken out of organisations. Furthermore public utilities which were traditionally College supporters were being actively privatised in the United Kingdom and they began severely to tighten up on their management development programmes.

It is also probably reasonable to say that in the early 1990s there was renewed competition from business schools in the United Kingdom, continental Europe and of course the United States of America. But whatever the reason the College discontinued these programmes.

5.9. Short courses

The discontinuance of the Senior Course and the General Management Course was compensated for by a number of other short programmes which were created by the College faculty. These courses were condensed into a shorter period of time and were often modular in nature. They included the New General Management Programme and the Strategic Management Programme. This was a period of some creativity for the College as new ideas were generated and marketed to those interested in management education and development. As always with this type of activity some of these short courses became successful and others were better regarded as experimental.

In time these activities were to develop into learning partnerships with clients and became an important stream of revenue for the College generally described as the Executive Education Division.

5.10. Tailor-made MBAs

Other innovations initiated at this time were the corporate or in-company MBA and the syndicated MBA. The corporate MBA was one which was designed specifically for a particular organisation, taking into account the knowledge requirements of the staff and how the organisation wished to develop its people. This type of programme was of course only available to large organisations due to its cost profile. At this time the College published what was a cross between a paper and a brochure on the topic of Corporate Universities, written by Wild and Carnall to indicate their interest in this line of business.

If an organisation was not large enough to be able to afford an MBA designed exclusively for them then there was an option whereby they could group together in a syndicate and an MBA would be produced which would suit the members of that group.

The College had some success in marketing this approach.

5.11. The nature of the College changes

What was actually happening during this period was that the College was increasingly moving towards being a graduate school of business which was becoming more and more reliant on the MBA programme. The MBA market was going to be of overwhelming importance to the future of the College and if this market were to weaken or shift then the implications for the College would be serious.

Of course as a Graduate School of Business the College was well placed to take advantage of research opportunities and the Henley Research Centre produced a steady flow of interesting research projects which brought both a material income and significant credits to the College. One of the most significant of these initiatives was the creation of the Knowledge Management Forum which created an opportunity for firms to work closely with academic researchers in order to solve real problems which they were facing at the time. This initiative continues to this day.

5.12. New degrees

Several new degrees were launched including an MBA in Information Systems Management and an MBA in Project Management. Neither of these degrees is available today.

In addition a new doctoral degree was developed, referred to as a Doctor of Business Administration or DBA. The DBA degree grew out of the debate which occurred between the Director of Doctoral Studies and a number of PhD candidates disappointed at the level of support which the College gave PhD research activity. Although there were a material number of PhD candidates at the College for some years the level of resources allocated to this activity were rather skimpy. Most of the individuals involved in research for a PhD were part-time mature students looking for a change in career and were unlikely to lodge any formal complaint. There were few full-time degree candidates and those who were registered as such often worked a considerable amount of time for the College on minor academic activities.

It was clear to the Director of Doctoral Studies that there were many unsatisfactory aspects to the programme and a discussion began as to how the situation could be improved. This resulted in the Director of Doctoral Studies putting forward a proposition for PhD improvements which was placed before the head of the Henley Research Centre. The improvements suggested in the proposition were considered to be far too expensive for the College, but it was decided that this type of enhanced programme could be packaged and sold as a high-priced doctorate mostly aimed at corporate executives. This approach became the DBA and was launched by Professor Arthur Money.

8. The DBA was launched under the leadership of the highly respected Professor Arthur Money during the Wild years.

5.13. The success of the DBA

9. Dr David Price spent more than a decade guiding the DBA programme during the Watson and into the Bones years.

When launched, the DBA was an immediate success with the College registering about 200 candidates in the first couple of years. From the point of view of the College, doctoral research was enormously labour-intensive. Each degree candidate required personal supervision. When the DBA was launched this meant one supervisor had to be found for each researcher. Of course today this has changed and the general practice is to have at least two supervisors for a doctoral degree candidate. But even with one supervisor for each research degree candidate it was not possible for the College to find an adequate number of suitably qualified supervisors.

But the concept of the DBA was so good that interest was shown by business schools abroad and shortly after it was launched collaborative activities were set up with the Singapore Institute of Management and l'Ecole Supérieure de Commerce de Grenoble. Neither of these two relationships lasted for any length of time. Nonetheless the success of the DBA led to the College's being involved in a European doctoral initiative referred to as EDAMBA i.e. the European Doctoral Association in Management and Business Administration. Through this organisation the Henley DBA received many accolades over the years.

5.14. The Henley Experience

The term the Henley Experience had been used in the College for some years. It referred to the ambience of the College and the hospitality offered to course members. There is no doubt that Greenlands was a strikingly attractive location both in terms of the stately home building but also its proximity to the river. The river is in its own right simply enchanting. It can also be quite refreshing just to sit and watch it flow by. In addition, the high standard of cuisine at the College was seen as a critical part of how the College presented itself. During the Wild years the Henley experience was strongly emphasised by those involved in promoting the College. This was especially the case with respect to the Executive Education Division which attracted senior managers to programmes at the College.

5.15. New faculty

During this period there was some minor change in emphasis as to the type of faculty which should be employed at the College and a couple of relatively visible international staff were was acquired. At the same time the College acquired a number of ESRC Teaching Fellowships and this programme allowed young aspiring academics to be attracted to the College, a number of whom were women and one of these individuals was to eventually become Associate Academic Dean of the College.

5.16. Overseas business grows

At this time the Distance learning MBA seemed especially to prosper. New markets were found all over the world. It is not clear exactly how extensive the international network actually was but in the 50th anniversary document it states that the College worked with individuals from 80 countries. In the same document it was claimed:-

Henley supported overseas students properly and in doing so has built up a tremendous international network which is bigger than that of any Business School. It has a physical presence with faculty and students in 23 countries, all closely quality controlled from the College[34].

It is quite probably true that by the mid-1990s the College was the biggest postgraduate MBA orientated business school in the world.

5.17. Degree-awarding powers

Having been established for 50 years and having thousands of Masters degree graduates pass through the doors it was reasonable to suppose that the College should have its own degree-awarding powers. There was no doubt that the College was highly respected for its MBA work and that it knew how to ensure that all the academic processes associated with such a degree could be executed efficiently and effectively.

There was of course another reason why degree-awarding powers were important. Although when I first arrived at Henley I had been told that the College was effectively the Business School of Brunel University this was actually untrue. The agreement between these two institutions was definitely an arms-length one as the College did not want to be subsumed into the bigger institution which constituted the University. As mentioned earlier independence had always been an important issue for the College.

As a result of this, since the early 1990s Brunel University had been developing its own Business School and was now ready to run its own MBA programme. Having two MBAs awarded by Brunel University was not going to be viable and therefore it was necessary for the College to seek its own degree-awarding powers.

On 19 March 1997 Masters degree-awarding powers were conferred on Henley Management College by the Department of Education through the Privy Council.

5.18. Equis acceptance

As mentioned earlier the College was conscious of the need to be accredited by the degree monitoring bodies and on 19 June 1998 the European Foundation for Management Development's Equis programme accredited the College, bringing more high visibility and prestige to the College's degrees.

---

[34] Internal report

5.19. New logo

It was decided that the College logo which had been in existence for quite a few years no longer reflected the new modern attitude of the College and so a new and more abstract logo was designed. The College colours remained green and the oak leaf was portrayed in a much more abstract way. Some members of staff regretted the absence of the acorns which were said to have a symbolic dimension associated with the growth potential which can be derived from learning.

5.20. An interesting incident

Despite the new structure and the high level of activity at the College there were still a considerable number of academics who were disgruntled. It is difficult to pinpoint specific reasons for this. There was a general feeling that the College was being run the same way as it had been under Kempner. There was of course a different king and the new king seemed to be sharing his power with the management team but there were still the barons. And of course, the king and the barons were overwhelmingly the most important members of the kingdom. The king and three of his barons were ex-Bradford.

One lunch time in the restaurant there were six of us at a table when a couple of faculty started actively to complain about some rather trivial matters. This went on for a few minutes when one of the others abruptly and loudly interjected. He demanded that they stop complaining about the College while consuming a "free" lunch made available by the College. This was done in such a dramatic way that everyone around the table just sat there in silence. Furthermore the griping of the individuals concerned was not heard over lunch again.

More generally the level of gossip and griping always seemed to me to be higher than one might have expected and I wondered if this was due to the fact that the faculty were able to take lunch in the dining room. Sitting around a table with colleagues who may not have had much in common, eating a so-called "free" lunch lent itself to discussing the institution and the people in it. It does not take much for this sometimes to become gossiping and griping.

5.21. The 4th Principal retires

Wild retired in February 2001 at which point he was 61 years of age. A number of members of staff looked forward to a fresh approach from a new Principal.

5.22. An assessment of the Wild years

Many of Wild's initial interventions into how the College functioned were regarded by some members of the College staff as rather superficial. At this time a senior member of faculty remarked to me that he wished the new Principal had not decided to have such a light touch on the tiller – a comment like this demonstrated that not everyone realised that Wild's first priority was to continue with the College on a "steady as she goes" basis. Wild did not reach the same level of innovation nor did he have the same entrepreneurial streak which Kempner had.

By the end of Wild's term of office the College had advanced significantly in some ways. It was now a truly global business with distance learning MBA degree candidates in many countries in the world. The MBA had also been developed for specific organisations and the College had begun to think about the corporate university world.

There had also been progress made in developing a wide range of short courses. The creativity of the faculty had been considerable in this respect. And there had been a significant improvement in the number of women members of faculty.

The Royal Charter, the application for which was initiated by Kempner, had come through and the College had been granted its own degree-awarding powers for taught Masters degrees. It was generally believed that in due course the College would obtain the right to award its own research degrees. There had been a considerable building programme and the capacity of the College had been enhanced. The work Wild initiated in refreshing the appearance of the College had been continued and the College looked well maintained. In effect the flow of innovations initiated by Kempner had been sustained by Wild. But Wild had not introduced any completely new ideas or approaches to the College business and therefore some members of staff did not regard his term in office as having delivered lasting value to the College.

The College had always been a registered charity and therefore it was never the intention that it should attempt to make substantial profits or surpluses. Thus during the Wild years the College made enough to pay its way. One of the established members of the faculty once described the College as being a competently managed small to medium-size enterprise which knew what it was and how it could behave. In the opinion of some members of staff by 2002 the College looked as though it was about to enter a *golden age* but of course this was on the assumption that it would continued to be managed in the same way as it had been up to that point.

Wild spent two terms of five years in office before a replacement was sought for the principalship. It appears to have been thought that there was no obvious internal candidate to take over this role. In fact there were a number of individuals in the College of whom it was said would make a suitable Principal. However for whatever reason these individuals appear not to have been seriously considered and as a consequence an outsider was sought to take over the role of the new Principal.

It is said in some management texts that one of the essential ingredients of successful management is the ability to pass on the baton when it is time to move on. This does not seem to have been done at the College. There was of course in this case a question of whether an outgoing Principal should have any say in his replacement. Some universities strongly oppose any attempt by an outgoing official to influence the decision of who will be selected to take on his or her role.

The Wild Years

Chapter 6

The Watson period

One wonders when Stephen Watson took over as Principal of the College on 1 March 2002 if he knew what a difficult act he had to follow. There had been a stream of innovation during the Wild years which would be a challenge to match. On taking up this appointment he was 59 years of age which is close to the age that the former Principals retired.

As mentioned in the previous chapter, at the time the 5th Principal was considering joining the College it was in most respects in good condition and its business was in a solid state. There was not yet reason to believe that the College was entering into difficult market conditions, which would within a few years precipitate a crisis. Finding a suitable potential Principal had been a challenge and the first round of searching led by the selection team had not produced any suitable candidates. Stephen Watson was selected from two final candidates after a second round of searching.

10. Professor Stephen Watson at a College Christmas Party.

Professor Stephen Watson was a distinguished scholar with an outstanding pedigree. He had been a founder member of the Judge Institute in Cambridge before going on to be a Dean at Lancaster Business School. Watson had much to offer the College.

Watson is described on the Emmanuel College website as being *an exceptionally talented academic who won a scholarship to Emmanuel in 1960 to read Natural Sciences, but came in to residence in October 1961 to read Mathematics. He became a Wrangler in 1964, and after Part III of the Mathematics Tripos studied for a PhD in Applied Mathematics. After winning a Smith's Prize in 1967, he was elected to a Research Fellowship of the College in 1968. Three years later Stephen became a University Lecturer in Operational Research and Statistics in the Department of Engineering and an Official Fellow of the College. In 1978 he became Head of the Management Studies Group in the Department of Engineering, and in 1986 was elected the first Professor of Management Studies in the University. He was much involved with the development of management education, becoming the first Director of the Judge Business School in 1990.*

Watson was a charming man who was clearly from the patrician classes. He was significantly older than the other Principals at the time of his appointment. He did not have much time to go to retirement. His appearance was that of a man who was very comfortable with himself and his performance. He did not give the impression of having much energy. He was a man with a balanced agenda and was noted for the fact that he had made enquiries from individuals who he had encountered at the College as to where he might find an interesting choir as one of his interests was singing.

Watson's appointment was welcomed by many at the College as there had been a growing realisation that the publication output of the academic staff needed to be increased and it was thought by some members of Faculty that he would be able to enthusiastically continue with the work already being implemented in this respect. Academics are always caught between the demands of teaching and research and because students' needs are often more immediate research output can suffer. It was thought that Watson's appointment would help stimulate the College's research efforts at the personal level and that the average number of papers published by faculty would improve.

It is also worth mentioning that Watson's appointment would bring a special level of prestige to the College. As mentioned before, Hall and Martin-Bates were Oxford men. Kempner was a graduate of UCL but Wild's original degrees were from Bradford[35]. With Watson on board the College was now being led by a Cambridge man with a perfect academic pedigree.

6.1. Expanding the management team

One of Watson's early moves as Principal was to enlarge the management team by bringing in additional College executives to whom he gave a voice concerning the direction of the College. This was a welcome move as it made the management team look considerably less elitist than it had in former years. Also much of the College's business had become even more complex in recent years and it was thought by some it might be advantageous to have more minds addressing the challenges the College now faced.

6.2. More accreditation

The next development Watson confronted was the formal accreditation for the College from the Florida based Association to Advance Collegiate Schools of Business. Although this had been initiated by Macmillan a few years earlier it was still no mean feat for the College to fulfil all the requirements. By obtaining recognition from this Association the MBA would be far more acceptable in the North American market.

6.3. Degree in coaching

With regard to new Masters degrees a Masters in Coaching was established. This had been built on top of a certificate in coaching which the College had been offering for some years and as such it was a natural extension of the College's activities in this field. It was recognised that there was an important community which wanted to have the professionalism of the practice of coaching reinforced through a programme of advanced academic study. It is interesting to see this as an aspect of personal development which can be traced back to the College's involvement with Belbin some decades earlier. This degree continues to be successful.

6.4. Executive Education

By this time Executive Education had become a major part of the College's business. The team behind this activity continued to develop and

---

[35] In the end Wild had three doctorates one from Bradford and two from Brunel.

market interesting events. Traditionally Executive Education was a term used for courses which did not lead to an academic award. But this was now changing and those who were attending training were interested in obtaining some sort of award for their efforts which had standing in the general world of business and organisations. This was one of the contributing factors to the creation of the Corporate University. The College promoted the idea of the corporate degree to a number of its major clients. Exec-Ed, as this activity now became known, constituted a major portion of the College's revenue. It was also regarded as a stream of income which was highly lucrative in the sense that it did not need as much servicing as distance learning MBAs.

6.5.   Loss of a significant member of staff

Professor Colin Carnall, one of the long serving faculty members who had come to the College with Kempner in the 1970s resigned and took up a post in a business school in a university. He had been an important player in the College for many years and it was even thought that he would become Principal. At the time of his leaving he had led the Exec-Ed Division for a number of years and his departure represented a significant loss for the College.

6.6.   The MBA market begins to shift

In the early 2000s business schools had been under pressure as the MBA degree was now being offered by a large number of universities. When Kempner brought the Henley MBA to the marketplace back in the early 1970s there were probably only a dozen other institutions in Europe offering such a degree. Thirty years later there may have been as many as 100 universities offering this degree in the United Kingdom alone. By any standards this represented a significant oversupply in the market.

Of course the College's MBA had a solid reputation in the market and this gave it a much higher degree of stability than was experienced by some other business schools. But the College's was an expensive MBA and there was no doubt that it would eventually come under severe market pressure. By 2003 the number of registrants for the MBA, although not growing, was holding up reasonably well.

6.7.   Important in-house MBA client leaves

One of the College's largest in-house executive MBA clients took its business away to another business school. This left a significant deficit in the budget which was referred to as the black hole and pushed the College into a financially distressed position.

6.8. Financial losses and Gainsharing

The black hole mentioned above resulted in Watson needing to warn the staff that it was likely the College would have a particularly unfavourable or poor financial year end. The immediate implication of this was that there would be no salary increases in the following year. In order to compensate for this Watson and his team introduced a Gainsharing programme[36]. This was effectively a bonus arrangement which was based on the College's ability to show an increase in performance primarily through cost control and it operated quite successfully.

6.9. Redundancies

However the College's financial situation became a matter of major concern to the Court of Governors. The College did not have deep reserves and it was not in a position to sustain a loss for any length of time and this resulted in a number of redundancies. In general the redundancies occurred among the non-academic and more junior members of staff.

The combination of the redundancies and improvements made by the Gainsharing programme returned the College to a positive financial position.

But perhaps more problematic, the entrepreneurial spirit with which the College had been managed by previous Principals appeared to have changed. It could be argued that the flow of innovation had been reduced.

6.10. The Watson interview

In an interview with Julie Davies of the British Library[37], available on YouTube, Watson points out that at Henley he was the Chief Executive of "a charity providing services to industry"[38]. It is not clear what the implications of this comment was, but it does suggest that in some way the College was not worthy of being considered an independent educational institution in its own right. If this was the case why was an august aca-

---

[36] http://simple.wikipedia.org/wiki/Gainsharing
[37] https://www.youtube.com/watch?v=c-H5LTErKbM
[38] The College had never been part of the main stream academic establishment but hearing it referred to as "a charity providing services to industry" seemed to be rather dismissive if not actually perjorative.

demic such as Watson working for "a charity providing services to industry". He admitted that Henley had been "very very successful" but that the challenge for the College was a strategic positioning issue and that there was tension between different parts of the faculty. He went on to say that at the time of his principalship the demand pattern for business schools was changing. In Watson's view the College should have merged with another institution but this idea was rejected by what he referred to as the Trustees. It is not clear from what Watson said why a "very very successful" institution should give up its independence.

In fact there had been a reasonable amount of speculation amongst the faculty concerning which other institution the College might try to do business with. It had been proposed by various individuals that Greenlands would make an excellent European campus for just about any of the big name business schools in the United States of America. However no one had any suggestions at all as to how such a relationship might actually work in practice. There was concern among some faculty that if a large American business school joined up with the College they would treat it as a venue and that the College staff would either be marginalised or made redundant.

6.11. Principal resigns and returns to Cambridge

During the last year or so of Watson's period as Principal there was a feeling that the College was not making as much progress as it could. It is hard to imagine how someone who thought he was the Chief Executive of "a charity providing services to industry" could have led the College to a better future. The thought was now planted that maybe the College should not be trying to function as an independent entity on its own and this may have affected the morale in the College.

It did not take long for the Principal to decide that he should return to his life fellowship at Emmanuel College in Cambridge. He therefore resigned before the end of his contract and departed. He had spent three years and ten months at the College. The press reported that "Henley Management College has begun its hunt for a new principal more than 18 months before the incumbent, Stephen Watson, finished his term of office, in December 2005"[39]. Interestingly Stephen Watson is to this day fondly re-membered when spoken of by some former colleagues; others only re-member him for his interest in singing.

6.12. An assessment of the Watson years

The Watson period demonstrated that the possession of an impeccable academic pedigree was not sufficient to ensure success as Principal of the College. Watson's short period as Principal is not remembered as being one of any significant improvements to the College. From Watson's per-sonal point of view it is not clear how much of a success he thought he had achieved. By the time he left the 'feel good' factor in the College was not high. The future was more uncertain than it had been before as there was now firmly established the idea that the College should be looking for a partner and thus perhaps a less independent future.

In fact Watson left the College in a reasonably sound financial state. The College management was more open with the enlarged team being re-sponsible for its day-to-day running. But there was the feeling that only quite limited progress if any had been made during his years at the helm.

On the positive side the College's good reputation in the business world continued. It was professionally and academically sound and its global presence was regarded by many as solid. But the flow of innovation had been reduced to a trickle.

By the end of the Watson period the number of women academics had increased significantly. Most of these individuals had come to the College as doctoral degree candidates and had stayed on to play a role in the run-ning of the College. There were also a number of women in the important course administration function of Client Director as well as Faculty Group Leader. The position of College Registrar was also held by a woman.

Just as when Wild retired, Watson did not leave any obvious successor. Finding a new Principal or Dean for a business school is often regarded as a difficult task and despite the beautiful work setting and the attractive package offered for this job, there was not a substantial list of candidates from which to choose the College's new leader.

---

[39] Times Higher Education - http://www.timeshighereducation.co.uk/news/todays-news/189363.article

The Watson period

Chapter 7

The 6th and Last Principal

11. Mr Christopher Bones.

On January 1, 2005 the 6th and last Principal of Henley Management College took up office. The appointment of Mr Christopher Bones created considerable interest at the College as he had neither an academic teaching nor an academic research background. On his LinkedIn page he states, *"Prior to leading a business school Chris worked in Industry for 22 years in mainly HR roles starting in Shell, moving to GrandMet, Guinness (and after they merged), Diageo and finally Cadbury Schweppes. He had an MA (Hons) from Aberdeen University in English/History."* Mr Bones was a high-flying executive of international standing with extensive leadership experience in some of the world's biggest and most famous companies.

The rationale for his appointment appears to be that the College wanted a captain of industry who would be able to lead them to new levels. There was probably also some realisation that the market for MBAs was shifting, the Exec-Ed market was hardening as it became more intensely competitive and a new approach was now required.

It has also been said by some members of staff that the change in emphasis in the type of Principal was a reaction to the previous incumbent. Stephen Watson had the perfect academic pedigree. Chris Bones had a

Master's degree from Aberdeen University[40] and no other academic qualifications.

Bones was an affable and engaging man. His manner and approach was considerably more informal than that of his predecessors. He was considerably younger than Watson. He was clearly energetic. He held strong views about how the College should change and he was keen to obtain support for his views. It is interesting that people perceived his management style differently but probably everyone agrees that it was fundamentally different from how the College had previously been managed by former Principals. He was relatively easy to engage in casual conversation.

Business schools are notoriously difficult to manage and the College had now become an even more highly complex organisation with more streams of business than many other business schools. There is an aphorism shared among those who know the university world which says that managing academics is akin to herding a flock of hens[41]. This amusing expression hides fundamental differences behind the mindsets of the academic and business manager. A search committee had been established to find the new Principal and there had not been a long list of applicants. Nonetheless the committee was convinced Mr Bones was the man for the job. In the event he was to spend three and a half years as Principal of Henley Management College before he became Dean of the Henley Business School at the University of Reading.

7.1.   The future for Henley

About three months after arriving at the College Bones presented his comprehensive vision for the future together with details of how the College was to be restructured and information about new roles and appointments.   This represented a root and branch rethink of the raison d'être of the College with a strong orientation to return to the original thinking of the founding fathers i.e. Hall and Heyworth, who had been driven by the need to offer facilitation to practising managers. Bones' vision was that the College should once again become the "business school for practising managers" and to do this radical change was needed[42].

---

[40] A MA degree from Aberdeen is a first degree. It is not the usual postgraduate award which it is at many other universities.

[41] Sometimes the term "flock" of cats is used instead of hens.

[42] As mentioned before there were those who had thought that Kempner's transformation of the College into a business school had been a mistake. These few individuals hankered

During the presentation, in which he outlined his strongly held vision of the need for extensive changes to the College's aims, structure and processes it was said that the College was a "great and successful institution". He assured those present that he needed everyone behind him and together they could make a significant impact and dramatically improve the circumstances of the College.

When I first read the transcript of Bones's vision of the future I wondered if he had read Noel Hall's speech in New York in which Hall had said,

> *The administrator's [43] business is to provide the conditions under which the work of the team can come to good effect in the achievement of some corporative purpose.*

> *The authorities are all agreed that there must be corporative achievement; more than one individual must be involved in the process. The higher executive is fundamentally the unifier. The process of administration is the process of unifying. But it is a team that has to be unified. A team is not simply an aggregate of a specific number of similar individuals. It is a carefully composed amalgam of different but complementary specialists. Nevertheless the amalgam has to be unified. The specialisms must merge in the group; otherwise the result is a rabble, not a team. Hence the importance placed in contemporary writing upon behaviour, group dynamics, human relations in their widest sense.*

It seemed that by calling for everyone to get behind him Bones was recognising the impact of Hall's vision above. Bones's degree was in history so he may have encountered Hall's thinking before. Getting everyone behind you is of course difficult to achieve especially in a university or business school environment.

7.2. New names for College structures

The Management Team was to be replaced by a significantly enlarged and more inclusive group of people to be referred to as the Operational Board.

---

after the "old days" when the College was substantially if not entirely focused on facilitating practising managers' self development. The strategy outlined by Bones after his three months in office referred back to this type of thinking.

[43] In today's language administrator would in this case probably be Chief Executive.

The faculty groups were to be reorganised as schools and different academic topics or fields of study were to be regrouped. The previous five faculty groupings introduced by Wild were reorganised as they were no longer considered to be appropriate. Bones's regrouping significantly changed the language with which these topics were normally described in a university environment. The groups which came into existence were now described as:-

School of Reputation and Relationships

School of Growth, Innovation and Enterprise

School of Projects, Processes and Systems

School of Management, Knowledge and Learning

School of Leadership, Change and HRM

12. Susan Foreman - the most senior female academic at the College.

It is not easy to know why this regrouping of topics could have made a positive difference to how the College functioned. It was of course done with a view to making the College offering more attractive to the business community. It is not known how it was perceived by the market or how effective it was. It did produce a challenge to some who are not familiar with the motivation behind these groupings and who therefore needed explanations as to why they better described the type of knowledge which was addressed under any particular heading.

At the same time Dr Susan Forman was promoted to the role of Associate Academic Dean which was the highest academic office a woman had held at the College. She held the post for less than two years.

7.3. Refurbishment of the premises

The property at Greenlands has been compared to an elderly but beautiful and very expensive mistress. It is very beautiful but it requires a very deep pocket to maintain in the way it should be kept. It was now thought that Greenands had been allowed to become run down and that the furnishings were in a poor state of repair. It was said that the College needed a substantial increase in double room accommodation. In addition it was necessary to refurbish some of the classrooms and syndicate rooms which had not been attended to for a few years. It was suggested that a substantial amount of funds would be made available for this purpose.

13. A degree awarding ceremony presided over by Mr Bones.

7.4.   Corporate Reputation

Much of the work had already been done in previous years by Professor Keith MacMillan to establish the John Madejski Centre for Corporate Reputation. It was now fully launched. This was considered a major achievement by everyone concerned and it brought a steady stream of influential individuals to the College. The Centre established an annual conference whereby celebrity speakers came to the College to give their insights into important reputational issues of the day.

7.5.   Some faculty members resign

The Principal encountered a number of cultural challenges. Perhaps because the mindset of the academic differs from that of the business manager there was a cultural mismatch between the way many of the senior academics had been led by a former Principal or Principals and the new approach which was now being taken. This resulted in a number of senior faculty members relocating to other institutions. Of course these individuals were replaced by highly competent personnel, but it is inevitable that in such a situation knowledge is lost when there is a significant degree of turnover among senior staff.

Some of the people recruited to replace the staff who resigned were very high fliers. However despite their business competence their impact on the College business did not immediately produce the results required.

The departure of so many senior staff appears to have created an unsatisfactory outlook or mood in the College and the Principal together with the new people who replaced those who left were unable to compensate for this.

7.6. The Information Systems

Another challenge faced by the new Principal was that of reorganising the Information Systems. Some members of the College admitted that the computer systems were rather old-fashioned and although they did the job they were by no means state-of-the-art and required updating. The Principal decided that it was appropriate to develop a new system capable of combining the traditional record keeping needed by the administrators (student records etc) with elements of e-learning desired by the faculty. When high-tech systems such as the ones proposed for the College are introduced there are often teething problems. The system chosen for the College produced some difficulties and the original estimates of the cost of this project were overshot. It is not entirely clear how much the project eventually cost the College, but the reality is that the system just did not work.

The overspend on this system put the College's finances into some distress.

7.7. Another new logo

In order to signal the new approach being taken to the College's affairs it was decided that another new logo should be developed and the College colours were changed from green to blue. It is not clear just how old the name Greenlands was. There seems to have been reference to it some 500 years before and it is clear that it was a most appropriate name to be given to the lush pastures surrounding the College buildings. As the site had been called Greenlands it was considered appropriate that the College colours should be green. However it was now decided that the College colours should become blue and the oak leaf was taken out of the logo.

It is also noteworthy that this new logo did not indicate that it represented a management education institution.

7.8. Beautiful pictures in a splendid book about the College

An interesting event of this period was the publishing of the book, *Henley and the unfinished management education revolution* by David Rundle. This is a beautifully prepared piece of work which traces the development of the College from its first beginnings to the date of publication. It is illustrated with some extraordinarily beautiful pictures which attempt to capture the spirit of Henley Management College as a Management Education and Development Institution. In the Preface of the book the Chairman of the Court of Governors, Paul Walsh said:

> *Henley Management College has a proud tradition and an exciting future. It may be the oldest management education institution in Britain, but it is also one of the most vital. An independent college with degree awarding powers, it has the flexibility and the vision to be a model of continuous development. It has repeatedly changed and been ahead of its time.*

What a lovely compliment to all the people who worked at Henley over the years.

But one of the interesting things about this book is that there is no mention in it of the MBA programme which had been the major driver of the College for 20 years[44]. It is of course unclear as to whether the author forgot to mention the College's MBA or whether he did not think it was a sufficiently important aspect of management education to be addressed in the book.

7.9. MBA registrations

As mentioned in the previous chapter the market began to shift and the number of MBA registrations at the College began to drop rapidly. There were two main reasons for this. The MBA market had now become highly competitive and questions were being raised as to how much real benefit an MBA delivered to an aspiring young manager. Specialist MBA degrees in Finance or Marketing were being offered and this was diluting this degree market. In addition to these major drivers the College re-

---

[44] The MBA and the MA from which it stemmed had been a feature of the College for 30 years but it was Kempner's introduction of the distance learning MBA which had transformed the College 20 years before.

viewed its relationship with its international associates who marketed the distance learning MBA abroad.

In the end the number of MBA registered students was said to have declined to approximately 3000.

7.10. Facilitation to practising managers

The Exec-Ed market had hardened and Bones's vision of the College becoming the *"business school for practising managers"* had become difficult to achieve. It was not easy to understand what the College had done so that it would be perceived as the *"business school for practising managers"*, any more than the many other business schools offering Exec-Ed courses. To achieve this, the College would have had to reinvent itself in a much more profound way and this would require a substantial amount of resources.

7.11. Accolade received

The Queen's Award for Enterprise International Trade was received by the College. The Queen's Award for Enterprise International Trade was applied for in 2005. It is a retrospective award based on the performance of the organisation over the previous six years.

7.12. The question of money and funding

One of the most interesting discoveries which I made while researching the history of Henley Management College was the fact that it survived the first 25 years of its life with minimal consideration of costs and how the institution would be funded. The fee which was asked for from course members was in no way related to the cost of operating the institution. During this period the management of the college had a minimal understanding of its operating or capital costs and as a result it did not have the controls in place which were necessary to ensure financial stability. It seems that when funds became low additional appeals were made. The lack of gravity associated with the cost and funding issue is well illustrated in the extract from the College Handbook in July 1945 shown in Exhibit 3.

Finance

The college will not be run for profit. Running expenses will be met by fees, but some support may prove necessary from the endowment income or guaranteed subscriptions. The capital will be covered by subscription. The control of finance will be vested in the court of governors.

The course is designed to last about three months, and fees will work out at about £100, covering living expenses and tuition. It is hoped to a reduction of fees in a limited number of approved cases may be found possible out of endowment income or guaranteed subscriptions.

July, 1945

Exhibit 3: An extract from a pamphlet produced by the College.

This situation had been rectified in the 1970s by Kempner who had been aware of the strategic importance of appropriate costing, accounting and funding. However during the years that followed, the cost of operating and maintaining Greenlands and all the staff required had grown considerably. This was especially true when high profile staff were introduced and high cost executive management was employed which had occurred during the Bones years.

Bones was of the view that the college was severely undercapitalised and this became a critical issue as the MBA registration numbers and the Exec-Ed programmes were not attracting the support which was initially planned.

Watson had at least to some extent anticipated the capitalisation issue when he argued that the College should be looking for a large partner. A few years into the Bones principalship this became a matter of urgent concern. The argument was that by joining a substantial university with a large undergraduate intake the College would have a firmer financial platform from which to function. Taking the location of Greenlands into account this made the choice of opening a conversation with the University of Reading about combining with the College an obvious one.

7.13. A merger is announced

It seems that the first public mention of the impending merger with the University of Reading occurred at a Special Meeting of the Court of Governors on 31 October 2007. At this time the University of Reading was mentioned as one of several possible institutions with which the College could combine. There had been many rumours circulating for some time and the name of an American University had been mentioned. However the logic of merging the two graphically adjacent institutions became compelling and work began on bringing them together. The full-time academic and administrative staff at the College were informed and meetings between the staff representatives and senior management from the University of Reading were held to ensure continuity of employment[45].

A press release was circulated on January 9, 2008 and some of the newspapers took up the story[46].

7.14. A meeting with the external faculty

In spring 2008 it was announced to the external or adjunct faculty that Henley Management College was going to merge with the University of Reading and a meeting was called where details of the merger were to be given to this highly diverse and dispersed group of people.

To me, and to some other members of the external faculty who had not been following the few mentions the merger had received in the newspapers, this news came right out of the blue and we wondered what it really meant[47]. One of my first reactions was to think that it did not seem to make sense to say that Henley Management College was going to merge with the University of Reading, at least not in the normal usage of the word merge. How could an institution with maybe 40 full-time permanent academics merge with another institution with maybe 700 or 800 or more full-time academics? Did the word merge not imply the bringing together of two entities of relatively similar size? Is it possible to merge a mouse with an elephant (even a relatively small elephant)? I wondered in what sense the word merge was being used and there is more to be said about this issue later in this chapter. The idea of a meeting was good news and no doubt all would be fully explained and we would then understand what was really going on.

---

[45] At the University of Reading members of the School of Business were briefed by the Vice-Chancellor.

[46] Financial Times http://www.ft.com/cms/s/2/7aaf8dd8-beaf-11dc-8c61-0000779fd2ac.html#axzz3SUXIMuGA ; The Guardian http://www.theguardian.com/education/2008/jan/09/highereducation.mbas

[47] I was to learn subsequently that in the Henley Management College Report of the Governors and Financial Statement for the year ended 31 December 2007 the intention of the Court of Governors to combine the College with the University of Reading was clearly spelt out.

The meeting was attended by about 40 or so part-time lecturers, mentors and tutors most of whom had been associated with Henley Management College for quite some time. A number of the old-timers like myself, whom I had not seen for a few years, turned up. There was certainly an air of anticipation about this event as we took our seats for the meeting in one of the College's larger meeting rooms.

We were to be addressed by some of the management team from the College and some senior members of faculty from the University of Reading.

7.15. The rationale for the merger

The meeting began with an address from the College's Academic Dean and not the Principal. He pointed out that Henley Management College was an important institution playing on a grand global stage. He made reference to how successful the College had been in former years and how the challenges which it now faced had materially changed. At this point in time the College was facing more intense competition than it had ever done before. He stated that as the College now stood it did not have the critical mass to be able to play the role that it wanted to. It simply needed to be bigger. It was for this reason that the Principal had decided that it should merge with the University of Reading. It was pointed out that the University of Reading had the resources which would allow Henley Management College to become a truly global player and to realise its proper role around the world.

No mention was made of the fact that the College had arguably been the original global business school with operations in some 30 different countries. It was not mentioned that the College had been independent for 60 years and that this independence was now being abandoned. No alternative strategies which might be available if Henley needed to engage in a strategic alliance with anyone else were discussed. There was no discussion of what was actually meant by the word merge and how this new association would unfold in the future. The merger with the University of Reading was presented as a done deal.

Following on from this presentation we were addressed by a leading academic from the University of Reading[48]. He said that he was very pleased to be involved with this merger with Henley Management College and

---

[48] It has been noted that neither the Principal of the College nor the Vice-Chancellor of University of Reading were present.

that he and his colleagues looked forward to a long and happy association between the two teams of people. Encouragement was the order of the day. The main message was that no one should feel threatened by the new arrangements being proposed. It was stated several times that after the merger it would be *business as usual*. The distinct impression which was given was that there was no intention of engaging in any major reorganisation.

At the meeting there was no suggestion that the College was in any financial difficulty but shortly thereafter the College gossip was that there was considerable financial distress.

7.16. Questions after the presentations

After these two presentations questions were called for. I thought we were now going to get to the bottom of some of the issues which needed to be addressed but I was rather disappointed. Questions were slow to come. A few relatively superficial questions were asked and rather vague answers were given. I thought that I should then ask what seemed to me to be one of the central issues on which this merger was being proposed. My question was that in light of the fact that Henley Management College was merging with the University of Reading because the latter had a much higher level of resources, what plans did the University have for investing in the new merged operation? Unlike previous questions this one did not elicit a vague answer. One of the senior team from the University replied and pointed out that there were no plans for any immediate investment from the University. So I wondered then what it meant when it was said that the purpose of the merger was to get access to resources from the bigger institution. But no further comments were made concerning this issue.

By the end of the meeting little explanation had been given and certainly there was no more understanding of what had happened to require this merger to take place. Furthermore we were not really any better informed about what was going to happen, but it was clear that the merger was imminent and that the senior executives of both Henley Management College and the University of Reading were pleased with the proposed merger arrangements.

It is of course impossible to suggest what the whole group felt, but speaking to individuals after the meeting the most common emotion expressed was surprise and dismay. Some people said that sixty years of hard work was now in some sense given away. I was actually surprised at how emotional this independence issue was for some people as organisations are well known to combine and change time and again over their period of existence. But there was concern among some of the external faculty that their livelihood might be lost as the new bigger organisation might no longer need their services. It is probably correct to say that mergers always lead to some degree of rationalisation. Some others aired the view that a large university would be more bureaucratic than the College had been. In my own case I was much more interested in the subject I was teaching than in the organisational issues of the institution at which I was working. I did not believe that it would make much difference to my work whether the College was independent or not.

There were some members of faculty and alumni who were sufficiently displeased at the prospect of the College's losing its independence to attempt to explore whether the merger could be stopped. It is not clear what grounds they felt there were for this but the Charity Commission was approached and it was not sympathetic to those who wanted to stop the merger. There was not enough strength of feeling for any other action to be taken and thus these grumblings came to nothing[49].

7.17. What did this meeting achieve?

On reflection this meeting of the external or adjunct faculty and the two senior members of University of Reading was quite significant. It demonstrated that neither the College nor the University of Reading had at that point fully thought out all the implications of the proposed merger. It also made it clear that neither side knew each other well. The comment about the possibility and yet at the same time the uncertainty of the future investment illustrates this. There was a lot of learning required by both sides and it was not going to happen in a flash.

Of course, this is how mergers normally begin to be operationalised and at least the external faculty now had a couple of faces which they could associate with University of Reading. The people from University of Reading were able to get some measure of the attitude of the College's external faculty which was of some considerable import to the institution. The external faculty were surprisingly loyal to the College considering

---

[49] *Up in arms over Henley merger*, by Ben Laurance, in Sunday Times Business News, 30 March 2008.

that many of them actually received only quite small amounts of work from the College. However nearly everyone in this group immediately realised that working with University of Reading was the only way forward.

7.18. Henley Business School comes into being

It was necessary to conduct due diligence and eventually the Principal held a party on July 31, 2008 to celebrate the last evening of Henley Management College. After drinks on the front lawn, those who attended were treated to a barbeque and a performance of Much Ado About Nothing performed by the Lord Chamberlain's Men at the river side. Staff were given a commemorative mug, and some sweets that were like sea-side rock candy with Henley stamped all the way through.

14. Souvenir mug handed out at the last night of the College.

The party celebrating the metamorphosis was attended by many of the administrative staff, but few academics were present.

Part of the merger arrangements was that the Business Faculty of the University of Reading would be folded into Henley Management College and that this new entity would be renamed the Henley Business School. On August 1, 2008 Mr Christopher Bones became Professor Christopher Bones, Dean of the Henley Business School at the University of Reading.

15. About 200 people came to the last night of the College celebration

7.19. An assessment of the Bones period

Bones's arrival at the College had been received enthusiastically. It was generally felt that the previous Principal had landed the College in what was the equivalent of the doldrums and that a breath of fresh air was required. The new Principal made a point of learning the names of all the staff including the gardeners and the cleaners.

Bones was noted by some members of faculty for a greater degree of inclusiveness which was demonstrated by the ease with which staff could have access to him. He made himself available at short notice to those who wished to consult him. He was perceived by some staff as devolving more responsibility to lower levels in the institution than other Principals had before him. He is said to have encouraged younger members of staff and to have given them recognition for their achievements when it was deserved. He participated in the teaching of some of the programmes.

16. Three Principals together in formal academic regalia at the college's 60th anniversary celebrations during the Bones term of office. Stephen Watson was noted for his absence.

The Bones period raises an important question for management and for governance which is, *Is it possible to appoint someone to run a business school who has no business school experience and little relevant education and no academic track record?* The answer to this is, of course, yes as this is exactly what happened. But can such a person be successful? This depends upon the objectives set for the incoming Principal. Some members of staff have said that the private agenda of the Bones appointment was to "get rid[50]" of the College. However this is belied by the Principal's opening address for the Future of Henley which was in some ways quite upbeat about how the College was going to improve its performance. Also Paul Walsh's comments in the Rundle book which most enthusiastically sing the praises of the College give no clue to there's being such a private agenda.

Thus ignoring the "get rid" of the College thesis, in his address to College members three months after his appointment in 2005, Bones asserted that the College needed to be radically transformed. He had a strong vision that the College should be profoundly changed. There would be few who would gainsay the fact that this was achieved. However considering that Bones had declared that the College was a "great and successful institution" it was never fully explained why this radical change was necessary. The College was not, at that point, growing rapidly but it was probably holding its own in what was a difficult market. But it appears that the ethos behind Bones's management was that the College was broke and that it had to be fixed.

Bones's plans were ambitious but he was unable to retain the support of many of the senior staff members, a large number of whom left the College. Thus he was not able to obtain what he asked for in his Future of Henley address when he said that he wanted "a commitment from everyone to get behind" his changes. Having such a large number of faculty move away from the College was not helpful to the Principal in this endeavour to achieve his vision for the institution.

The MBA market was rapidly maturing and the College came under severe financial stress with losses in the MBA registrations and more difficulties appeared in developing the Exec-Ed market than Bones and his team had envisaged. Exec-Ed was much more lucrative for the College but the financial attractiveness of this activity made it highly competitive.

As already mentioned the idea that the College should in some way combine with another institution had already been sown by the previous Principal. Watson had not managed to achieve this but it was possible that his

---

[50] "Get rid" is clearly an emotive term. What is probably being said by those who use it is that there was an interest among the Court of Governors to transfer the responsibility for maintaining the College as an educational institution to another larger entity. As pointed out here this is very speculative and contradicts the early statements made by the Principal and the Chairman of the Court of Governors.

thinking had prepared the intellectual path which his successor was now to follow and to make Watson's original suggestion reality. Having the College join the University of Reading meant that Greenlands would continue to be a centre of excellence in management education. It was also believed that joining the University of Reading would keep the Henley Management College brand alive. The University of Reading's Whiteknights Campus was 10 miles away from Greenlands. The range of degrees and programmes it offered did not overlap much with the College's and thus it was seen as a good fit and the approach by Bones to merge with them was welcomed.

17. Greenlands changes hands as one flag is lowered and another is raised.

A small number of former College staff and former students felt hurt by the College's loss of independence which they believed was not the only way forward for the College[51]. There was talk of assembling a private rescue package for the College but this did not materialise.

The new institution offered a more comprehensive range of educational services and degrees in the field of management education. This new entity has gone on to become a top rated business school not only in the United Kingdom but also on the world stage.

The question of whether the interests of management education in the United Kingdom were well served by combining these two institutions is

---

[51] *Smith sticks oar into Henley dispute*, The Sunday Telegraph, Sat 19 January 2008

seldom asked. The answer to this question depends upon one's perception of the value of diversity. As I do not believe in the value of diversity for its own sake and looking at what has been achieved in the six years since the merger the answer is for me, Yes!

The name Henley Management College was removed from the register of charities on 20 November 2008 and on 16 March 2011 the Royal Charter was surrendered.

Chapter 8

Did the fat lady sing?

8.1. International acclaim

When I started out on the interesting and enlightening journey of writing this book, a former colleague said to me *Who are going to be the goodies and the baddies in your story?* I was surprised by that question at the time and my surprise has not abated. There are no goodies or baddies in the story of Henley Management College. Some Principals were extraordinarily innovative and effective and their work resulted in the College becoming a world class pioneer in management education. Other Principals were less so. Alas, not all Principals are equal and the six different Principals which the College had all faced quite different challenges and opportunities. Nonetheless there are several salutary lessons to be learnt from what transpired over the 60 plus year life of the College.

Few organisations can claim the success this College enjoyed. For 60 years it was the leader in various aspects of management education at which it excelled. It had a remarkably loyal following from its staff and from business people who had any contact with it. But the success as described in this book was of a delicate kind and the College needed a particular strategy which was difficult to conceptualise and to implement. This strategy was rooted in innovation and entrepreneurship, especially in social entrepreneurship.

The College's ability to innovate was recognised early in its existence on both sides of the Atlantic. A paper[52] published by New York University pointed out:-

> *The most interesting educational experiment in the world today for the student of comparative administration and business and*

---

[52] The administrative staff college: executive development in government and industry, (1950), Marshall E. Dimock, New York University

government is the Administrative Staff College at Henley-on-Thames, England. This College is pioneering the methods which, in any industrialised nation, are needed to restore the flexibility and initiative that must always accompany free enterprise. The College also provides a new approach to leadership training in that enrollees are recruited in fixed proportions from public and private employment by a method that produces balanced management teams among the members (as the "students" are called), and the teaching procedure stresses group work and self instruction rather than formal lectures.

8.2.   New pedagogy

The College was instrumental in breaking new ground in pedagogy related to management education by introducing a form of problem-based open-ended learning, supported by managers being required to reflect on what they knew and what they had experienced, thereby sharing and cross-fertilising with others. This approach developed both professional and personal skills in the course members as well as allowing them to understand the need for thinking about their own development over the coming years. This combination of effects is what the syndicate approach was really about and why it was such a powerful way of encouraging improved organisational performance. Although a similar approach had been practiced for some time by the Military Staff Colleges, Hall and colleagues pioneered its use in the world of civilian management education and this brought the educators from the Commonwealth and elsewhere to their doorstep to learn how it should be done.

Of course the advantage of being a first mover often does not last for long especially when there is a truly enormous pent-up demand for the product or the service. The two-year waiting list for a place on the Course clearly indicated among other things - *beware this is an interesting market and you won't have it all to yourselves for long.* In practical terms this meant no matter how hard Martin-Bates worked at promoting the College's original Course, he could not stave off the incursions which the competition was making into his market. If it was to survive the College needed the university connection which was delivered by Kempner.

8.3.   New delivery mechanism

The College's success in using distance learning as a means of delivering an MBA degree was the envy of the academic world. For its time the number of registrations it obtained was simply extraordinary. They were certainly world leaders in this approach to education.

Kempner's timing in entering the distance learning MBA market can only be described as inspirational. It completely transformed the College. It was now de facto a business school. The distance learning MBA provided it with the resources necessary to develop the new generation equivalents of the original Course conceived by Hall and his colleagues back in the 1940s. In turn these new courses further opened the executive education market in which the College enjoyed considerable success.

8.4. Strength in the market

Wild's work in consolidating the College's position and obtaining degree-awarding powers and various accreditations truly strengthened the market presence of the College.

But in the same way as the creation of the London and Manchester Business Schools signalled the end of the College's dominance in the mid-career management development market, the arrival of scores of universities offering MBA programmes would inevitably have an impact upon the distance learning MBA business. And the distance learning MBA was the seam of gold which underpinned the financial success of the College. Losing sight of what was happening to the primary revenue stream has to be seen as a questionable act.

It would be incomplete not to mention the College's income from research as well as the DBA. Much good work has been done in both these fields. Some excellent research has been completed at the College even going back many years to the Belbin days when personnel and team performance and competencies were the main topics of research interest. The DBA was brilliantly conceived and excellently delivered. However the college was essentially an institution whose raison d'être was learning in the form of courses and taught degrees.

8.5. Success in the future

What was then to be done to survive in the 21st century?

There is only one answer to this question and that is there was a critical need for a continual stream of relevant innovation. The innovative ideas had to be taken up by academic leaders with entrepreneurial skills and converted into new products and services, which both aspiring and practising managers wished to acquire. Of course this implies that the organisations for which such people worked or intended to work would see the value of these products and services.

But this advice is reminiscent of the fable of the Owl and the Centipede. "The owl was the wisest of animals. A centipede with 99 sore feet came to him seeking advice. 'Walk for two weeks one inch above the ground; the air under your feet and the lack of pressure will cure you,' said the owl. 'How am I to do that?' asked the centipede. 'I have solved your conceptual problem, do not bother me with the trivia concerning implementation,' replied the owl[53]".

It is hard to know whether it would have actually been possible to retain Henley Management College as an independent entity or whether circumstances had changed so much that it was better to regard it as having had its day. Its past glory was not going to pay its way in the future.

But with the creation of Henley Business School perhaps the fat lady had not sung? The achievements of Henley Management College were to be given a new lease on life within the University of Reading context.

8.6.   The ultimate test?

It is part of the academic DNA to create hypotheses and to test them so as regards the fat lady the following hypotheses are relevant:

Would the founding fathers and/or the early Principals have aspired to create a management education entity as successful as Henley Business School is today? It is difficult for me to believe that they would not be very pleased with what exists now. HBS is regarded by both academe and industry as one of the top business schools.

Could the College have achieved this on its own without the support of a large and important University? The answer to this question is that it is most unlikely. The current operation is twice the size of the old College; the resources required to grow to this extent were just not available to the College and it was very unlikely that an independent College could have raised these funds. It is perhaps very ironical that the College was never

---

[53] Shubik M, A Game-Theoretic Approach to Political Economy, The MIT Press, USA, 1988.

well funded and this became a critical issue after it started to employ expensive executives as it did from the middle of the first decade of the 21st century.

Would the founding fathers and/or the early Principals believe that the independence of the College was of the utmost importance? This is a much more difficult question but I believe not. In the Journal of the Greenlands Association published in 1963 Sir Hector Hetherington is quoted as having made a remark of central importance to understanding management education and the position of the College therein. He said, "For the final objective of all this enterprise is not theory but rather practice directed to the fuller service of the public interest". In most respects the public interest was well served by the merger of these institutions.

We can sometimes lose sight of the fact that all education in our society is ultimately a public interest issue. Henley Business School has made itself into a significant player which supports the public interest by furthering the efficiency and effectiveness of business practice in our society. This was achieved not only by the courses it offered and the researches it conducted but by the pedagogical understanding it developed and practised.

Did the fat lady sing?

Chapter 9

And then the Phoenix – Henley Business School

On August 1 2008 Henley Business School became an operational entity. The event was described in its promotional material as follows *Henley Management College merged with the University of Reading to create a new world-class business school, Henley Business School. The merger brings together two highly complementary business education offerings. Henley Management College has long been a leading international provider of executive education and MBA programmes, while the University of Reading Business School has been a world leader in international business research, with centres of excellence in business education for the financial and real estate markets. Together they will constitute one of the largest and best business schools in Europe, offering a full range of programmes and a powerful combination of academic research and thought leadership.*

18. The modern offices of Henley Business School at the Whiteknights campus.

And then the Phoenix –
Henley Business School

The last few years of the independent College had indeed been difficult but it is an ill wind that blows no one any good and this story ends with the creation of a new business school which will quickly go on to be a leader both in the United Kingdom and on the world stage. Still, the first few years after the merger were challenging as it did take time for Henley Business School to find its feet and to move forward as an integrated academic entity. Christopher Bones left the University of Reading in autumn 2010 to assume other academic and consulting interests. Professor John Board took up the post of Dean of Henley Business School.

John Board had spent a number of years as the Director of the ICMA Centre (Finance) which was one of the Schools of Business at the University of Reading, which he joined after being on the faculty at the London School of Economics. He had a solid record in both teaching and research and he was highly regarded in both academic and professional business circles. On taking up his appointment he identified a number of objectives, not least that of ensuring that the Henley Business School is seen as the successful next stage in the Management College's development, together with more prosaic tasks, such as ensuring a continual improvement in the Business School's position in the various ranking surveys.

Management studies had been part of a University of Reading offering for quite a number of years. The first programme in management had been offered as far back as the 1960s through the Department of Economics. Of course management is important to engineers and thus the Department of Construction created a Management Unit which also provided some management courses but this was on a rather low scale basis. By the end of the 1990s however other parts of the University had begun to teach management in one form or another and a range of bachelor and masters by course work degrees were being offered.

But it was only in the early 2000s that the University began to consolidate its academic interests in management studies and created the Reading Business School. The Reading School of Business was an umbrella entity for five academic disciplines which were Management, ICMA Centre – (Finance), Real Estate, Economics and Accounting. Although they were independent of each other they all had some common intellectual overlap. By this stage there were approximately 100 members of academic staff in the Reading School of Business and 1100 students of which about 620 were undergraduate and about 470 were post graduate. About two thirds of the students were home-based and one third were from overseas. For the University it was a relatively small scale activity but it had growth potential and it was highly regarded.

In addition to teaching activities academic research had been important at University of Reading and each of these disciplines had strong reputations in this respect. There was also a significant PhD programme. In general University of Reading had a depth of expertise and a high degree of acceptance in the academic community. University of Reading's administrative systems were also highly developed.

The University of Reading did not have an MBA or a DBA programme and it was not especially active in the Exec-Ed arena.

It is clear that the activities of these two management education entities did not overlap and that there was an opportunity for synergy when they worked together.

It is arguable that before the merger neither the College nor the Reading School of Business had an adequate critical mass but combined they constituted an entity that would have an undisputed presence on the global management education stage. The College had nearly always been global but in truth it had been thinly spread.

19. University of Reading investment has ensured that Greenlands remains a highly attractive site.

With the resources now available to it, and several million pounds have actually been invested in bringing the School's facilities right up to date at both Greenlands and Whiteknights, Henley Business School has prospered. Enrolments have increased, Exec-Ed is growing and research has also increased.

Henley Business School's overseas interests have considerably expanded.

Henley Business School describes the strategic impact of the merger as having brought together the complementary post-experience provision of the former Henley Management College and the pre-experience provision of the then School of Business of the University of Reading into a full-service business school, from undergraduate education to board-level development. The aim was to integrate and blend the capabilities of both institutions into an organisation of significant scale and reach, and to develop an investment programme that would leverage what was already world-class and to close the gaps in those areas where previously neither institution competed effectively.

20. On a fine day Greenlands look like it will be there forever.

And then the Phoenix –
Henley Business School

In terms of all the important accreditation and ranking systems Henley Business School is now ranked as one of the highest in the world. It has been singled out for its excellence in teaching, research and student care. So what is the story of Henley Business School and how does it relate to Henley Management College? On page 1, I mentioned that Henley Management College had been built and developed on *a solid stream of significant innovation.* I have also pointed out that it had to reinvent itself a number of times as the environment changed. By the time Martin-Bates retired the College was quite different from what he had inherited from Hall. Kempner virtually turned the whole place on its head. And more innovation happened when the College joined hands with University of Reading and the Henley Business School came into existence. Henley Business School is a composite of the original thinking which dates back to Hall, Martin-Bates and Kempner and the work of the many individuals at University of Reading who pioneered management studies at that University. It is today conscious of this rich heritage which is reflected in its attitude toward its teaching and research programmes. This is evidenced by the fact that the HBS MBA is built on a conceptual framework which emphasises the need for degree candidates to achieve a high level of personal development as well as acquiring professional skills appropriate to the work place. Furthermore in this MBA degree Henley also emphasises the need for a balance between academic and professional understanding and achievement.

Perhaps to end this story it is appropriate to ask the question, Is Henley Business School as it is now constituted, the final form it will take? It is a rash individual indeed who thinks that he or she can see far into the future - but it is the stated intention of the current Dean of the School that, whatever form it takes, the spirit of the founding fathers of the College which emphasised self development, collaboration, cross-fertilisation and reflection, will be preserved and enhanced.

And then the Phoenix –
Henley Business School

HMC to HBS Timeline

From Administrative Staff College to Henley Management College to Henley Business School

The following is a list of some of the more significant events which occurred between 1942 when the idea of a college was first mooted and 2008 when Henley Business School became operational.

The events which are described during the Wild years are not necessarily perfect chronological order. This was a very active time for the College and the innovations which were being generated often occurred in parallel.

Every attempt has been made to include all the major events.

Date	Event	Comment
1942	Concerned industrialist, civil servants and others begin a discussion on how to create an Administrative Staff College in the UK	A number of members of this group of people became members of the Court of Governors when the Administrative Staff College was incorporated.
October 1945	College Incorporated as Administrative Staff College at Henley-on-Thames	➤ Company limited by guarantee and not for profit. ➤ Court of Governors established with Geoffrey Heyworth as Chairman. ➤ The target for the covenanted appeal target was established at £45,000 pa
August 1946	Principal appointed and Greenlands selected and leased (subsequently purchased) from Lord Hambleden	Noel Hall takes up his position of Chief executive of the College
April 1947	Director of Studies Appointed	Mr D B Hoseason. He died in 1948 following a motor crash
1947	Greenlands developed to a point where it was acceptable as a venue for a management course	College not yet able to take the 60 course members as originally planned

Date	Event	Comment
March 31 1948	First course began	Three course sessions held. College informally opened by the PM, Clement Attlee
	Courses a success from the point of view of the members but financially problematic	The direct running costs of the College not covered by income
	➢ Courses oversubscribed and a waiting list established ➢ Waiting list grows to two years	
	Interest shown in developing Administrative Staff Colleges abroad	➢ India, Pakistan, Australia, New Zealand to mention only a few locations. ➢ Many locations visited by College staff and this was funded by the Ford and the Liverhulme Foundations
1953	Conference of past attendees from 15 sessions	Request to increase direct instruction especially on financial matters
1954	Hall visits Commonwealth countries	Support from Commonwealth countries strong
1955	➢ Greenlands Association ➢ The power of the alumni is appreciated	Marks 10th anniversary of the incorporation of the College
1957	➢ Knighthood conferred on the Principal. ➢ Duke of Edinburgh visits the College ➢ Hall becomes the first Ford Distinguished Visiting Professor at New York University	Sir Noel Hall
1960	➢ Courses continue to be oversubscribed. Review course introduced ➢ Senior Conferences being held	Very small expansion to the College's educational activities.

Date	Event	Comment
August 1961	Principal resigns after 15 years' service	Sir Noel moves on to the position of Master of Brasenose College. New Principal James Patrick Martin-Bates
1962	➢ Growing demand for Course places ➢ Proposal to build a second college declined by Court of Governors	➢ College unable to satisfy the demand. Waiting period to be admitted on a course becomes 2 years. ➢ Applicants for courses turned away
1963	The Franks Report	Recommended the establishment of Business Schools in the UK and led directly to the creation of London Business School and Manchester Business School
1965	Building and operational costs exert financial strain on College	Martin-Bates' appeal for funding from the Foundation for Management Education not as well received as hoped for
1966	➢ Initiated by Martin-Bates Tavistock Institute evaluates the Course ➢ London and Manchester Business Schools commence with competitive programmes	Result of the review was generally positive but some updating was required to the form of delivery of the Courses. Too much reliance on syndicate work
1967	➢ Computer based business game called the Executive management Exercise ➢ New course on Quantitative Methods	➢ Introduced Belbin's group performance theory Belbin's work becomes important as to how syndicate groups are compiled. ➢ The results of research in this leads to a considerable stream of research and course work for the college.

Date	Event	Comment
1968	General Management Appreciation Course	A three week event for older corporate executives which would grow into a longer programme. This course would eventually be renamed the Senior Course and continue to run until the 1990s.
1969	➢ Civil Aviation Courses ➢ Nominations on the main course began to decline	Tailored courses for a specific client. This was the first step in the Executive Education domain.
1970	➢ London and Manchester Business schools obtain funding from University Grants Committee ➢ A link with a university reconsidered by Governors	
	Directing International Operations course introduced	The College takes advantage of the availability of Sir James Lindsay the former Chairman of Metal Box India.
1971	➢ Search for Martin-Bates' successor begins ➢ Governors look to fining an individual who could simultaneously be the College Principal and hold a professorship at an appropriate university	
October 1972	1	➢ Third Principal appointed ➢ College becomes an Associated Institution of the University of Brunel	Professor Thomas Kempner who would also be co-opted to the University Senate as well as being an ex-officio member of the Court of Governors

Date	Event	Comment
May 1974	➢ Brunel Masters Degree MA launched ➢ This degree was later renamed as a MBA Increase in academic faculty to meet the needs generated by new courses.	➢ Four residential modules of seven weeks ➢ A substantial number of overseas students
1974	Henley Centre for Forecasting	Financially independent of the College
1976	➢ Henley Management Development and Advisor Services (HMDAS) ➢ First computer purchased	➢ This service lead to the College acquiring in-house Executive Development work ➢ The computer chosen was from a manufacturer called Prime
	➢ The Trade Union View of Industrial Relations	Short course
1977	Expansion of research activates	The number of research degree associates reach 65
	➢ General Management Appreciation Course renamed The Senior Course and becomes a flagship event	
1979	➢ Internal professorships established ➢ The Centre for Employment Policy Studies established	
1980	Part-time MSc taught by Henley staff at Brunel	
1980	➢ Scholarships for Women in Management ➢ Head Teacher Scholarships also offered	Aimed at women who had not been selected by their firms to attend and therefore would have to fund themselves.
1981	Distance learning is placed on the College's agenda	

Date	Event	Comment
	Administrative Staff College name formally changed to Henley – The Management College	
1982	Brunel Senate approves the use of distance learning programmes	
1984	➢ Henley Centre for Information Management established ➢ Personal computers introduced into syndicate rooms	
1985	Henley Distance Learning Limited established	College retains nearly 50% of this business. Outside investor hold the rest.
	New Henley Management Course introduced in a modular form and which incorporated some aspects of distance learning	
1987	Distance learning MBA numbers exceed 2000	
	Increase in administrative staff to meet the success of the Distance Learning MBA	
1988	PhD enrolments expanded	
	Staff grows considerably	
	Flat management structure with no faculty structure	
1990	➢ Principal retires ➢ Active Distance Learning MBAs estimated at over 7,000	After 18 years service

Date	Event	Comment
April 1 1990	➤ Fourth Principal appointed ➤ The appearance of the College is that of a rather tired building which the new Principal sets about modernising. ➤ College procedures modernised ➤ Blue room opened to all staff ➤ Reception modernised ➤ Dining room self service ➤ Officer-men serving at annual dinner changed ➤ Access and parking at College regularised	Professor Ray Wild
	➤ Introduced The Management Team ➤ Divisions and then ➤ Faculties	➤ Birchall, Carnall, MacMillan, Tom Taylor etc ➤ MBA and Executive Programmes, Research Divisions ➤ Info Ops, Marketing, Finance, HR etc
	Overseas Distance Learning MBA agents expanded	
June 28 1991	Royal Charter Granted	
1991/1992	Enrolments on the Senior Course and the GM Course decline and both these course are eventually abandoned	
1992	Doctor of Business Administration established and the demand quickly exceeds the Colleges ability to cope	
	EDAMBA and EUDOKMA	

Date	Event	Comment
	Project Management Masters introduced	
	Information System Masters Introduced	
	Brunel starts its own business school	
July 1995	Application for Royal Charter for Degree-awarding Powers	
	Centre for Board Member Effectiveness established with an annual conference	
	Knowledge Management Forum developed as a subscription group of companies promoting research into KM applications	
	College accredited by AMBA, and EQUIS	
March 19 1997	Power to awarded Masters degrees is conferred on Henley Management College which is the new name assumed.	
June 291998	Admitted to Equis	Accreditation to the European Foundation for Management Development
February 28 2001	Principal retires after 11 years service	
March 1 2001	Fifth Principal appointed	Professor Stephen Watson
	Management team expanded	
	Master degree in coaching established	
	Enrolments on MBAs begin a steady decline	
2002	AACSB International -The Association to Advance Collegiate Schools of Business	Accredited by US body

Date		Event	Comment
		The College loses a major client.	
		Henley's ability to remain an independent College is questioned.	
		There are financial concerns and there are involuntary redundancies among the more junior staff.	
		Gainsharing is introduced to the College	
2003		It is decided to re-arrange pension funds provisions.	
2004		The College is not considered to be making the progress that it should.	
2004		Principal resigns before the end of his contract. Watson subsequently announced that while at the College he saw himself as the Chief Executive of "a charity providing services to industry".	
January 2005	1	Sixth Principal appointed	Mr Chris Bones
		The new Principal is welcomed enthusiastically.	
		A root and branch programme of change is announced.	
		A woman is appointed to a senior academic position as Associate Academic Dean	
		Henley's official colours are changed from green to blue	
		Syndicate and conference rooms refurbished	

Date	Event	Comment
	Introduced Schools as the main organisational structure	Project Processes and Systems are to be changed
	Academic groups which are now called Schools are renamed.	
	Management team to also be renamed and expanded	Operational Board
	MBA course of study is redesigned – MBA 5	
	John Madejski Centre for Corporate Reputation fully launched and became active	
2006	Henley and the unfinished management education revolution published	David Rundle writes for Henley Management College
2006	The Queen's Award for Enterprise International Trade	
2007	The suggestion of Watson's that the College cannot survive as an independent entity is revived.	
	Organisations which might be interested in acquiring the College are approached.	
	Bones negotiates the merger of HMC and UoR	
July 31 2008	Principal holds party attended by approximately 200 people to celebrate the last evening of Henley Management College	
	Bones becomes a Professor and the Dean of Henley Business School – University of Reading	

Date	Event	Comment
August 1 2008	Henley Business School operationalised	The Faculty of Business Studies of Reading University is re-named Henley Business School and resources of Henley Man-agement College become the Greenlands Campus of that in-stitution.
November 20 2008.	Henley Management Col-lege removed from the register of charities	
Autumn 2010	Christopher Bones resigns as Dean	
October 1 2010	New Dean appointed at Henley Business School	Professor John Board, an inter-nal appointment, took up the post of Dean of Henley Busi-ness School
March 16 2011	Henley Management Col-lege's Royal Charter sur-rendered	

Principals and Chairmen

Date	Chairman of the Court of Governors	Principal of the College
1944	Geoffrey Heyworth	
1946		Noel Hall (15 years)
1961		JP Martin-Bates (11 years)
1963	Duncan Oppenheim	
1971	David Barren	
1972		Thomas Kempner (18 years)
1976	Alex Jarratt	
1989	Denys Henderson	
1990		Ray Wild (11 years)
1996	Roger Hurn	
2001		Stephen Watson (3 years)
2004	Paul Walsh	
2005		Christopher Bones (3 years)

Bibliography

Cornwall-Jones, A, (1985), *Education for leadership*, Routledge & Kegan, London.

Chilston Viscount, (1965), *WH Smith*, Routledge & Kegan, London

Hall, N, (1958), *The making of higher executives: the modern challenge*, School of Commerce, New York University,.

Martin-Bates, J, (1963), *The Administrative Staff College in the UK and in developing countries*. The Administrative Staff College, Henley-On-Thames.

Remenyi, D, (2014), *MBA voyage of discovery, deep down the rabbit hole*, Academic Conferences, Reading.

Rundle, D, (2006), *Henley and the unfinished management education revolution*, Henley Management College, Henley-on-Thames.

Slater, H, (1988), *Henley at Greenlands*, Henley-The Management College, Henley-on-Thames.

Taylor, H, (1968), *The Administrative Staff Colleges at home and overseas*, Lyon Grant and Green, London.

Urwick, L, (1944), *The elements of administration*, Harper, New York.

Urwick, L, (1947), *Comparative organization*, Manchester Municipal College of Technology, Manchester.

Index

Lightning Source UK Ltd.
Milton Keynes UK
UKOW07n0634080915

258259UK00002B/2/P